1,00

The author of this book has, as a Shakespeare scholar, the advantage of having gone through a unique school; he has translated into German Shakespeare's Sonnets and eighteen—so far—of his plays. Moreover he is an experienced man of the theater, author of two plays that were successfully produced in Vienna, and student of stagecraft at Max Reinhardt's Theatrical College.

His double capacity of translator and producer enables Mr. Flatter to advance new and convincing explanations of the various problems in *Hamlet* that have long perplexed students; the puzzle of the hero's "inactivity," of his so-called "failure," the mystery of the dumb show, performed in addition to the spoken play-within-the-play, the question of

HAMLET'S FATHER

how deeply the Queen is implicated in the murder, of why the Ghost appears in the closet scene and what the purpose of his appearance is.

Mr. Flatter approaches the problems of the play from the point of view of Hamlet's father. It is the Ghost who, in his opinion, is the motive power; it is he who sets the action moving, and it is he who, before he returns to the grave, achieves his revenge.

Mr. Flatter presents a strong case for a play that is entirely logical, closely knit, and unified in action and psychology.

BY THE SAME AUTHOR

Shakespeare's Producing Hand

A Study of His Marks of Expression to Be
Found in the First Folio

David Garrick as Hamlet
(From a print in the Harvard Theatre Collection.)

HAMLET'S FATHER

BY

RICHARD FLATTER

His forme and cause conioyn'd, preaching to stones,
Would make them capeable.

III. 4

NEW HAVEN
YALE UNIVERSITY PRESS
1949

ERRATA

p. 21, line: *for* Do *read* do.

p. 121, line 16: *for* The following *read* the following.

p. 130, line 1 (first word): *for* Shakespeare *read* Hamlet.

p. 127, line 3 of the footnote: *for* are *read* art.

p. 152, line 10: *for* of *read* or.

p. 203, footnote: *for* Heinemann *read* Heinemann and W. W. Norton.

CONTENTS

APPENDIX

ILLUSTRATIONS

NOTE TO THE READER

WHEN picking up this book and seeing its title—*Hamlet's Father*—many a reader will murmur: "Aha, yet another book on Hamlet! Yet another solution of the mystery! For surely this title, this dragging in of Hamlet's father, can merely be meant to serve as a red herring?"

Let me say at once that the reader is perfectly right. Yes, this is yet another book on *Hamlet,* yet another attempt to solve the enigma that has puzzled so many before. And yet it is equally true that I am going to deal firstly, mainly, and lastly with Hamlet's father; for it is my submission that the Ghost is not only Hamlet's father, but also the father of the play. He, by his desire to be avenged, sets the whole action moving; he instructs his son and imposes on him the duty of revenge; he intervenes in person when, in the Closet-scene, the flow of the lava threatens to take the wrong direction; and it is he who in the end achieves his victory: the victory of justice over secret evil.

True, the Ghost will sometimes disappear from sight; just as he does in the play, so in this book also. For it will be necessary, in order to find the way out of the labyrinth, to inquire into several problems, such as:

> *How deeply is Gertrude implicated in the crime?*
> *What had her connection with Claudius been in the past and what is it now?*
> *Does the King, and with him the Queen, see the Dumb-show?*
> *If she does, must she not take it that by the play-within-the-play her husband has openly been exposed as the assassin of old Hamlet?*

vii

These and other questions will have to be examined before the central problem of the play can be tackled, which is, *why the Ghost appears in the Closet-scene and what the purpose of his appearance is*. It is in that scene that the various rays, reflected from his wife, his son, his brother, are concentrated as if in a burning-glass. The result may well be—at least it is hoped—that this dead and insubstantial figure, emerging from darkness and resolving into darkness, will be recognized as what he truly is: one of Shakespeare's most human creations.

*

THE GHOST'S PART IN THE PLAY

In the modern theatre, before the curtain rises, we are
wont to study the programme. From it we learn that
Mr. So-and-so will be seen in the part of "Duncan, King
of Scotland", that two rather unknown young actors will
represent "his sons", and that Mr. X and Mr. Y will be
"Generals of the King's Army". Thus when after some
preliminaries Mr. X and Mr. Y appear we know that
Macbeth and Banquo have entered—even had we never
heard or read anything about the play and its contents.

At the Globe Theatre it was different. True, play-bills
were not unknown; they were written or, in later years,
even printed. In 1587 a Master John Charlwood registered
at the Stationers' Office his exclusive right of printing
"all manners of Billes for players". Such "bills" were put
up publicly and distributed by hand. Yet they gave
merely a rough outline of the play, a very much abridged
argument, such as we find on the title-pages of certain
Quarto editions. The play-bill announcing a performance
of *The Merchant of Venice* was probably much the same
as its title in the Quarto of 1600:

> The most excellent/Historie of the *Merchant/of Venice*.
> With the extreame crueltie of *Shylocke* the Iewe/
> towards the sayd Merchant, in cutting a iust pound/
> of his flesh: and the obtayning of *Portia*/by the
> choyse of three/chests.

Another bill, put up on a public "post", might have read
as the title of the Quarto 1608 reads:

> M. William Shak-speare:/His/True Chronicle Historie
> of the life and/death of King Lear and his three/

Daughters./With the vnfortunate life of Edgar,
sonne/and heire to the Earle of Gloster, and his/
sullen and assumed humour of/Tom of Bedlam.

Such advertisements were intended to rouse interest
in the play, not in the players. No announcement was
made as to who was to play whom. No list of characters
was given from which the relations between the persons
on the stage might have been deduced.

Shakespeare had no other means of announcing his
characters but to introduce them by word of mouth. With
one or two exceptions (which, however, only seem to be
exceptions) he takes great care that his audience should
recognize the chief characters for what they are at the
very moment of their appearance. Especially as regards
the hero of the play he hardly ever allows him to enter
unheralded. To achieve this he usually employs two or
more people (introduced sometimes for no other than that
purpose) who in a few sentences speak of the protagonist
and prepare for his entry.

In *Coriolanus* the play begins with "a Company of
Mutinous Citizens", and no later than in line 7 we learn:

First, you know Caius Marcius is the chief enemy of
the people. . . . Let us kill him, and we'll have corn
at our own price.

From line 27 onwards we hear more about the man we
have not seen yet:

Would you proceed especially against Caius Marcius?—
Against him first: he's a very dog to the commonalty.
—Consider you what services he has done for his country?
. . . he pays himself with being proud . . . he did it to
please his mother. . . .

When later ("Hail, noble Marcius!") the hero himself

2

comes in we know already something of his mind and manners.

Before in *Julius Cæsar* the hero himself makes his appearance he is talked about at great length:

> . . . we make holiday to see Cæsar and to rejoice in his triumph.
> —Wherefore rejoice? What conquest brings he home? . . .

In *Antony and Cleopatra* there are not more than 13 lines before the two enter. In these few lines, however, we are told:

> . . . this dotage of our general's . . . like plated Mars . . . upon a tawny front . . . the fan To cool a gipsy's lust. . . .
> The triple pillar of the world transformed
> Into a strumpet's fool. . . .

Similar devices are employed in *Romeo and Juliet*, in *Timon of Athens*, in *Macbeth, King Lear, Othello*, and other plays. In each case the chief character is spoken of, and thus introduced, before he appears in person.

*

Turning now to *Hamlet* we find that when the play begins two supers come on to the stage, shortly to be joined by another super and a minor character, Horatio. It is obvious that, true to pattern, they are introduced for the sole purpose of introducing somebody. Whom? We should assume that they are to pave the path for the hero of the play. As it turns out, they introduce the Ghost.

It would of course be reckless to rush to the conclusion

3

that the Ghost of Hamlet's father is the chief character of the play. Still, it seems somewhat strange that just in this play Shakespeare should have deviated from his normal and well-established method, thus misleading his audience into assuming that now, after those preparations, it must be the chief character who makes his entry. The Ghost who enters instead will be taken by no one to be the real hero. All the same, a certain incongruousness remains: Will not the audience expect Hamlet's father to play a part commensurate to the momentous manner he has been announced and brought in? On the other hand, if he is meant to be a minor character only, is not his introduction a little too elaborate?

This query leads straight to the question: what is the Ghost's part in the play? Is he an active participant in the cut and thrust of the action? Or is he merely a residuum of the antecedents that went into the making of the play? In the former case, should he not appear and intervene more frequently? In the latter, would it not have been possible to do without him altogether?

Actually there is one version of *Hamlet* in which the Ghost never appears. This is the French version, given at the Comédie Française, first performed on September 30th, 1769. It held the stage for more than forty years. Its author, M. Jean François Ducis, brought the play rigorously down to the three unities of Time, Place and Action. Gertrude had been an active party in her husband's murder; she speaks openly of her guilt; she refuses to marry Claudius and wishes Hamlet to succeed his dead father to the throne; Ophelia is not Polonius's but Claudius's daughter; Claudius is slain by his nephew; Gertrude kills herself; Hamlet survives them and we are given to understand that he will marry Ophelia, who never lost her five wits nor ever attempted to drown herself. The play, despite of all that, was performed under the title *Hamlet* and its author was called "Shakespeare".

4

The last to personify its hero was the famous Talma. M. Ducis himself was made an "Immortal".

In this version, as already said, Hamlet's father never appears. We learn all about his fate while listening to conversations on the one hand between Claudius and his trusted friend and accomplice Polonius, and on the other between Hamlet and his friend Norcestes. Only once, in the third act, Hamlet, in sudden excitement, declares that he sees his father; but neither Gertrude nor Ophélie, who are with him, nor the audience are allowed to catch a glimpse of the apparition: it exists merely in Hamlet's imagination or hallucination. Evidently M. Ducis was of opinion that the Ghost belongs to the preliminaries of the play, not to the play itself; so he cut him out altogether. For him Hamlet's father had no part in the action.*

Not so for Shakespeare. For him it would never have done to inform us of the King's murder as he informs us (to take the nearest parallel) of the death of old Fortinbras: he lost his life in single combat with old Hamlet—and we learn what there is to be known from Horatio, who tells us about it. About the succession to the throne and of the event of the marriage we learn from Claudius's speech in I. 2. About Hamlet's sea-voyage we learn from his letters and from his report to Horatio. It all goes to show that in this play as in others Shakespeare makes good use of the device of narration, and we may assume that also in the matter of old Hamlet's death he would have found means of telling us all that is necessary for us to know. Obviously, however, he did not wish to leave that part of the story to narration, nor let the Ghost appear as narrator only. He wanted to employ him as an active participant in the play. And so the question obtrudes itself once more: does not the Ghost appear too seldom and intervene too little?

In fact, neither is true. His appearances in the first act

* See Appendix, Note A.

5

are frequent; there is also the Closet-scene. And in between and even after his last appearance, can we ever say that he ceases to be there? He is there not in person, but in principle, so to speak; not visible all the time, but all the time perceptible—by the task he has laid on his son's shoulders. Not before the very end, when all is over, does the Ghost cease to act. He is the originator of the task—and what happens with that task, its ups and downs, the near miss, the near fulfilment, that is the play.

The motive of the play is the Ghost's; and in this sense it may be said, it is his play.

If we look at Hamlet's own performance, his hesitations, his scruples, his delays, we may think it either a good or a poor performance; that depends on whether we feel inclined to regard him as active or inactive, as strong or as weak. Yet if we look at the Ghost's performance, what a difference! There can be no doubt that he achieves a most magnificent success. In the face of so many and various difficulties and obstacles he succeeds in obtaining his revenge.

A dead man, his body buried and entombed. His soul lodging in purgatory, allowed to walk as a mere spectre certain hours of the night only. Murdered in unsuspicious circumstances. Not the slightest rumour has been breathed during these months. No witness alive. The murderer himself enthroned as king, which means that he is practically beyond jurisdiction. His widow, whatever her part in the crime, in her new husband's power. Even had old Hamlet actually returned from the undiscovered country and regained life, in some way similar to Juliet who awoke in her coffin (if such an idea can, for a moment, be entertained at all) he would have been confronted with insuperable difficulties. Having no witnesses, how could he have hoped to convince even a single soul that he was not stung by a serpent, but poisoned by the present king? And had he, instead of proceeding in accordance with law

6

and order, simply acted and run his sword through Claudius, what would have saved him from being hanged and quartered as a regicide?

Yet although he is what he is, an insubstantial apparition, coming up from the shades, he is firmly determined not to return to his everlasting home before he is avenged. The obstacles do not deter him. During the first two nights of his walking he merely succeeds in attracting the attention of two unimportant officers. He walks a third night; and this time Horatio comes to meet him. Horatio, the scholar, tries to make him speak; they try, all three of them, to hold him back; they even strike at him, but he vanishes. He is resolved to talk to one person only, to his avenger. On the fourth night his son at last comes. Now he could speak, and yet there is still another obstacle: witnesses are present. So he rather risks the loss of all he has gained so far, and beckons his son to follow him. Will he do so? There is no knowing beforehand. All the same he refuses to speak; only when Hamlet, despite the dangers of death and hell, tears himself from his companions and follows the apparition to that lonely spot, only then does he speak to his son and calls for his revenge.

Considering his mental energy and moral determination we must admit that old Hamlet, despite the frailty of his incorporeal existence, is not only worthy to be spoken of worthily, but still worthy to play a worthy part. He not only "was a man, take him for all in all", but he still is that man—a man, able to partake in the action that follows his revelation. And he takes that part.*

*

No, it hardly seems justified to say that the intro-

---

* Tradition has it that it was Shakespeare himself who at the Globe Theatre impersonated the Ghost of Hamlet's father.

7

duction of the Ghost is too elaborate. On the other hand, how is Hamlet himself introduced? Do people, before he enters, speak about him, his mind and manners, as they do about Macbeth, or Othello, or Romeo? The queer fact is that he is introduced in a very scanty way; one could almost say he is not introduced at all. At the end of I. 1, in the last few lines, Horatio suggests:

> Let us impart what we have seen to-night
> Unto young Hamlet. . . .

He thinks that to him the Ghost might speak. Marcellus agrees; he also knows, he adds, where to find the prince. That is all. In I. 2 Hamlet enters with the King, the Queen and all the others, without any further introduction. No one of course will say that Hamlet is not the chief character of the play. Still, the difference between the ways in which Hamlet the father and Hamlet the son are introduced makes one think.

*

The two tragedies of *Macbeth* and *Hamlet* show in more than one respect a special affinity. Either play is about the murder of a king; in either case the murderer is brought to justice and receives his punishment. In the case of *Hamlet*, however, Shakespeare so to speak acts as counsel for the prosecution; in the case of *Macbeth* as counsel for the defence. In the first case he looks with the eyes of the avenger, and the criminal, Claudius, is kept more in the background. In the second case he is more concerned with the murderer, Macbeth, and it is the avenger who is kept in the background.

In either case it might just as well have been the other way round. We can imagine a play (called *Malcolm* instead of *Macbeth*) in which the same story would be treated from Malcolm's point of view. Left behind burdened with the task of avenging Duncan's death, he would try to find out who has murdered his father, to bring the criminal to trial and to inflict on him the retribution he deserves. Throughout such a play Malcolm would be in much the same position as Hamlet is in this: the avenging son would represent his dead father; he would, as it were, continue his father's existence, impersonate his father's spirit or, if we prefer the expression, his father's ghost.

Now, it could be said, is not that what Malcolm actually does, i.e., in the play as we have it? That is true. Malcolm may for long stretches disappear from sight; but he for whom he stands and the cause for which he acts are never lost sight of, until in the last act the English Army, led by the avenging son himself, approaches, bringing step by step nearer for Macbeth the end, for Duncan the revenge.

In one way, it is true, the play of *Macbeth* is more transparent: in it, justice comes back full circle. Duncan had not only been robbed of his life, but of his throne also. He himself, being dead, cannot be restored to his former position; but his son, who has inherited his kingly rights, is reinstated. At Scone, at the same place where Macbeth had crowned himself, the final act of restitution will crown the play: in his very last words Malcolm invites his kinsmen to see him "crowned at Scone".

(Had Shakespeare lived a hundred years later he might have written a play on Oliver Cromwell. At the end of that play he would, we may assume, have shown the triumphant return of the beheaded Charles—represented in his son.)

As much, then, as *Macbeth* may be said to be Duncan's play, just as much may *Hamlet* be called the Ghost's play. In either of them it is, in the end, the principle of justice that emerges victoriously. To speak, however, of the "principle of justice", thus substituting an idea for a

9

person, an abstract term for the reality of life, tends to obscure the facts. Who, in truth, is it that brings the punishment down on the guilty heads? Is it Malcolm in the one case, Hamlet in the other? Does either of them act for himself and on his own behalf—or is it not rather that both are mere instruments in others' hands?

In fact, it is not Hamlet with whom Claudius is struggling throughout the play, but the Ghost. Claudius does not know what Macbeth had to learn to his horror: that the murdered are not dead; that they rise again

And push us from our stools.

Claudius never meets the Ghost nor ever hears anything about him; and yet, when in the end he falls at his nephew's hands it is—not in reality, but in truth—his murdered brother who kills him.

*

THE QUESTION OF GERTRUDE'S INTELLIGENCE

IN a Hamlet production in which I had a hand, the Queen, throughout the play, behaved in a peculiar way: When sitting beside her husband she held her head erect, gazing in front of her, as if unconcerned with his presence. She never glanced at him, not even on those rare occasions when she had to address him. She gave the impression of being estranged from her husband, hardly on speaking terms with him.

I do not mean to say that this interpretation of Gertrude's relation to Claudius is the only correct one; but I do mean to say that it is a possible interpretation. It may even be that it conforms better to the text than the attitude usually adopted by the stage Gertrudes, that of a loving and submissive wife. On that point more will have to be said later. First, however, the question demands an answer: what kind of woman is Hamlet's mother?

The critics regard her as an easy-going, self-indulgent, weak woman, a combination of moral indolence, folly, and harlotry. Sir E. K. Chambers* considers her to be "unable to realize her own moral degradation". Granville-Barker† describes her as a "shallow, amiable, lymphatic creature". Dr. A. C. Bradley‡ says of her that "she had a soft animal nature, and was very dull and very shallow". However they vary in detail, on one characteristic all the critics seem to be agreed: on her lack of intelligence. It is this point that calls for investigation and, I should think, modification. Only then can the question be tackled as to what share she had in her husband's crime.

*

* In his edition of the play in *The Warwick Shakespeare*.
† In his *Prefaces to Shakespeare*, Third Series: *Hamlet*.
‡ In his *Shakespearean Tragedy*.

Gertrude is a liar. An adulteress cannot help telling lies. Especially in this case we should keep in mind that for a queen, always surrounded by courtiers, waiting-gentlewomen and servants, it must have been difficult enough to deceive her husband. That she succeeded in doing so is the first piece of evidence against the assumption that she is a fool.

As to her other lies: fools tell foolish lies and are easily found out. Gertrude, however, tells lies that are so subtle that through centuries she has deceived not only her partners in the play, but audiences, readers, and critics alike.

(1)

At the end of the Closet-scene Hamlet exit, "tugging in Polonius", and with "Enter King" the next scene has begun. There is—in the Folio—no interruption, one scene develops into the other. There is only a few moments' pause during which Gertrude weeps; it is this sobbing Claudius refers to when he says:

There's matter in these sighs, these profound heaves.

Having remained on the stage, Gertrude cannot possibly know anything about Hamlet after he had left her. And yet, when Claudius a short while later asks her: "Where is he gone?" she not only tells him that he left "To draw apart the body he hath kill'd", but adds:

. . . he weeps for what is done.

That is a lie.

Hamlet has not wept for Polonius. Immediately after he has killed him he sneers at the "rash-intruding fool"; and when he returns to him in order to "lug the guts into the neighbour room" he again has only sneers for the

12

"foolish prating knave". Neither in text nor context is there any indication that Hamlet shed a single tear for Polonius. Why, then, does Gertrude tell that lie? Because Hamlet is her son, and her lie is a white lie.

(2)

A bigger lie is Gertrude's report on how Polonius met his death.

When after the Closet-scene Claudius asks: ". . . how does Hamlet?" Gertrude answers:

> Mad as the sea and wind when both contend
> Which is the mightier: in his lawless fit,
> Behind the arras hearing something stir,
> He whips his rapier out, and cries "a rat, a rat"——
> And in his brainish apprehension kills
> The unseen good old man.

The master liar never tells outright lies; he shows his art by relating facts that are perfectly true in themselves, only that he perverts the truth by omitting certain features of it. Nothing Gertrude says is contrary to the events as we know them. Hamlet did kill the old man; he did cry: "a rat, a rat!"; he whipped out his rapier and he did hear "something stir behind the arras". Yet she does not say why the old man stirred: she omits to say that she herself cried for help and that Polonius merely took up her own cry. She omits these details for one reason: she does not wish to tell her husband why she felt her life was so seriously threatened that, against the agreed plan and against all wisdom, she had to cry out for help. Now, what was it that gave her this feeling of mortal danger?

Let us first reconstruct the psychological situation at the beginning of the Closet-scene. When Hamlet enters

13

his mother's room he is now sure that the Ghost's words were true, i.e., that, Claudius is a murderer. He knows moreover that Claudius now knows that he, Hamlet, knows. Up to the performance of the Mouse-trap the two had to keep on tolerably good terms, at least outwardly; now the two enemies know: death is inevitable. The question for either is only: will it be death for the other or for himself? Hamlet, only a moment before, could have killed his enemy; but he had spared him. He himself is no assassin, but he knows Claudius to be one. He murdered his own brother while his victim was asleep: why should he hesitate to dispose of his nephew whom he now must regard as a constant danger to his life?

Of all that Hamlet is fully aware. From now on, he knows, he must always and everywhere be on the qui vive against a dagger-thrust or some other attempt on his life— even here in his mother's room. For the next few minutes, he knows, there is no danger: he has left the King behind, kneeling in prayer. At present, therefore, his deadly foe cannot be in the room; but at any moment he may come in—and then he might need his sword.*

That, I think, is the situation as it appears to Hamlet when he enters. But now, what makes his mother cry out for help, apparently in genuine fear for her life? Her actual words are:

> What wilt thou do? thou wilt not murder me?
> Help, help, ho!

Bradley describes the scene like this:

> . . . when, on her attempting to leave the room, he takes her by the arm and forces her to sit down, she is terrified, cries out, 'Thou wilt not murder me?' and screams for help.

---

* In *Der Bestrafte Brudermord* Hamlet asks expressly whether the door is locked.

14

Professor J. Q. Adams (in his edition of *Hamlet*, 1929) describes the procedure as follows: The Queen

> haughtily starts towards the door. Hamlet seizes her and draws her back. She struggles. He forces her into a chair.

Professor J. Dover Wilson (in his book *What Happens in "Hamlet"*) explains the action like this:

> He seizes her by the arm, and forces her roughly into a seat. At this she naturally takes fright, and calls out to Polonius.

I cannot persuade myself that this explanation meets the case. Nobody ever was killed by being forced, however roughly, into a chair. Why, then, should Gertrude be afraid for her life when treated in that way? I do not say that Hamlet did not force his mother into a seat; he did, but three lines earlier. He says:

> Come, come, and sit you down, you shall not budge:
> You go not till I set you up a glass
> Where you may see the inmost part of you.

It is evident that the forcing into a seat takes place in the first of these lines: "Come, come, and sit you down." How is it, then, that she takes fright only two lines further on? Granville-Barker gives the following comment: Gertrude

> finds herself in his hard grasp and flung back in her chair again (where she had enthroned herself to receive him), and next so menaced by the fierceness of his

> > you shall not budge;
> > You go not till I set you up a glass
> > Where you may see the inmost part of you . . .

15

that she cries aloud for help. It is not that threat which
frights her, but plainer danger. For despite him, and as
he feared, the "soul of Nero" is astir in Hamlet. And did
not Polonius from his hiding echo her cry and draw
the frenzied rage upon himself, the sword-thrust that
dispatches him might truly, in a moment more, have
been for her.

I refuse to believe that Hamlet, even in his most
frenzied rage, would ever have killed his mother. And just
here where he clearly speaks of his intention to "show her a
glass", i.e., to preach her a sermon, there is nothing to
indicate that all of a sudden the "soul of Nero" should
have taken possession of him. In any case, it is useless to
speculate whether or not Hamlet might have lifted his
sword against his mother, had Polonius avoided betraying
himself. The question, to put it once more, is rather this:
what is it that frightens Gertrude so much that she cries
out for help?

I submit the following interpretation. Hamlet wishes
his mother to sit down; he bids her do so twice: "Come,
come, and sit you down" and later again: "peace, sit you
down". Why does he insist on that? Because he wants to
"set her up a glass". What does he mean by that? He
means what he actually does shortly afterwards, introducing it with the words:

> peace, sit you down
> And let me wring your heart. . . .

That "setting up a glass" and this "wringing her heart"
mean the same, namely the comparison between Hamlet's
father and Gertrude's present husband.

Here now Professor Dover Wilson asserts that the two
pictures Hamlet invites his mother to compare are full-
length portraits. Yet the idea of two such portraits
hanging on the wall of the Globe Theatre (which wall?)

and of Hamlet and Gertrude standing there with their backs to the audience, scrutinizing the paintings, whereas Shakespeare says twice: "sit you down"—all that is more than improbable. I feel convinced that it is miniatures that Shakespeare had in mind.*

Now, in order to show his mother the two miniatures side by side, holding his own in one hand and grasping his mother's with the other hand, Hamlet must either sit by her or bend over her or kneel at her side. As she is seated with her back to the background—the most natural position for her—he too would have to turn his back towards the entrance. That, however, he cannot dare, or he would expose himself to any attack that might come from that direction. In his situation, physical and psychological, he cannot risk being unprepared. So he draws his sword in order to have it at hand should he need it. Certainly he has no other intention but to lay the sword beside him or simply to have it drawn and ready for any event: she, however, fears he is about to attack her— and cries out for help.†

This exposition seems to meet all the requirements of the situation. It seems to explain Gertrude's mortal fright ("thou wilt not murder me?") and also why Hamlet insists on her being seated.

Returning now to Gertrude's report we find that she tells Claudius a lie by suppressing two points: (a) that Hamlet drew his sword and, at least in her imagination, threatened to murder her, and (b) that it was she who cried out for help first. Once more, as in the previous case, she colours the facts. And she has the cunning as well as the presence of mind to do so.

---

* See Appendix, Note B.
† In Quarto 1 we find the following:
  Queene: How i'st with you?
  Ham: I'le tell you, but first weele make all safe.
—which obviously means that Hamlet does something to make sure of his own safety.

17

(3)

Gertrude's biggest lie, however, is the version she gives of Ophelia's death. She smothers the truth under the flowers she heaps on the poor suicide.

There can be no doubt that the water did not come to Ophelia and drown her, but that she went to the water and drowned herself: argal, she is guilty of her own death. The grave-diggers have learned the details of the case from the coroner; so they must know what they are talking about:

> . . . if this had not been a gentlewoman, she should have been buried out of Christian burial.

Hamlet at once notices the "maimed rites" and draws the obvious conclusion:

> This doth betoken
> The corse they follow did with desperate hand
> Fordo it own life.

Finally there is the priest. Surely it is his duty before arranging for a burial to inquire into the circumstances of the person's death? And in this case, that of the Prime-minister's daughter, he is not likely to have acted negligently. Yet he on his part says frankly:

> And, but that great command o'ersways the order,
> She should in ground unsanctified be lodg'd. . . .

His words make it clear that the King has overruled the ecclesiastical law and commanded a Christian burial, which otherwise would never have been granted. The priest does not expressly speak of suicide—he uses the euphemistic expression: "her death was doubtful"—but his references to the "great command" and to the "shards, flints, and pebbles" that otherwise would have been thrown on the coffin, show unmistakably that he regards himself as officiating (much against the grain) at a suicide's burial.

Nowadays a coroner would of course pronounce that the Lady Ophelia committed suicide while the balance of her mind was disturbed. When dealing with a Shakespearian situation, however, we have to put the clock back and judge the case as it would have been judged then. For the Elizabethans Ophelia's death was suicide; there is no getting away from that fact. Suicide it was not only in the grave-diggers' and the priest's eyes; King and Queen also accepted it as such, or they would not have tolerated the "maimed rites".

Professor Dover Wilson is, as regards Ophelia's death, in two minds. On p. 262 of his book he says: "Ophelia goes mad and drowns herself"; on p. 265, however, he has the following:

> I am not suggesting that Ophelia *was* a suicide, only that the Grave-diggers' altercation, the maimed rites and the churlish priest's words make the funeral that of a suicide; it is the atmosphere not the fact that matters.

"How shall we find the concord of this discord?"

Seeing, then, that all concerned (the Court, the Church, the grave-diggers, even Laertes) are agreed on the fact of suicide, how is it possible to reconcile the event with the story as told by Gertrude? The answer is, it is impossible. If Ophelia really tried to clamber up a tree to hang her weeds on a bough and if, while doing so, she fell into the "weeping brook" because "an envious sliver broke", who, even in those days, would have thought of denying her the honour of a Christian burial? What Gertrude describes is an accident. Such a death, caused by a sheer mishap, cannot possibly be called "doubtful", as little as the

death of a bricklayer who fell off a scaffolding because of
a broken board. Had Gertrude told the coroner and the
priest what she has told Laertes, no one would have
spoken of suicide. But to those authorities of state and
church she obviously reported a different version, namely
the truth: that Ophelia went to the water and drowned
herself.

There is yet another reason for our assuming that
Ophelia actually commits suicide. It is, we know, one of
Shakespeare's artistic habits to write variations: a given
theme is repeated in contrasting and complementary
shapes and forms. The relation between Lear and his
daughters is contrasted with the relation between Gloster
and his sons; and there are numerous other instances.
Hamlet's very first words of self-revelation sound the
theme "self-slaughter", later repeated in "To be or not to
be". What he considers and reconsiders, devoutly wishes
for and yet rejects, is executed by Ophelia unthinkingly,
and therefore unhesitatingly. Conscience makes him a
coward; but she has no conscience any longer; her will is
not puzzled—and she goes.

Here now a suspicious reader might ask whether I wish
to suggest that Ophelia went into the water "wittingly".
That, according to goodman delver, would "argue an act",
and that in its turn would mean that she is far from being
as mad as we usually assume her to be. Am I really going
to say that she had lucid moments and that she drowned
herself knowing what she was doing?

It is, I admit, not impossible to see Ophelia's case in
that light. The text does hardly disallow it. I have had
the impression sometimes as though Ophelia, while
distributing the flowers, were arranging her own funeral.
And her last words:

God ha' mercy on his soul.
And of all Christian Soules, I pray God. God be wi' ye.

Do not show very much madness; they rather sound like a farewell for ever. Indeed, if an actress were to speak those words as if taking leave of this temporal world, she could easily create the impression of being just about to shuffle off this mortal coil. Yet I think that would be going too far; it would dangerously modernize the psychological make-up of the play. At Shakespeare's time psychiatry was still in its infancy: madness did not exclude suicide and suicide was no proof of madness. Argal: although Ophelia was a lunatic, everyone regarded the way she ended her life as suicide.

*

Evidence that Ophelia's death was meant to be regarded as suicide can be found in *Der Bestrafte Brudermord*. In this early German version of *Hamlet*, based probably on an adaptation, taken to the Continent by English travelling actors (in 1626 a company of English players performed a *Hamlet* tragedy at Dresden), Ophelia, we are expressly told, commits suicide: she throws herself down from a mountain top.

*

Now, however: why does Gertrude so highly colour her story that the true fact almost disappears under the verbiage? Is it that Shakespeare wants to insert a piece of rhetoric? Some aria for the enjoyment of those who appreciate poetry for poetry's sake? There is no such thing as poetry for poetry's sake in Shakespeare, at least in his mature work. There, everything is subordinated to the emotional relations between his characters. These psychological threads that never cease to be spun from one person to the other, this emotional cobweb is the only unity to be found in a Shakespeare play. But this cobweb unity is stronger than any other, far stronger than the three classical unities combined.

What, then, is the emotional relation between Gertrude and Laertes? She is afraid of him. It was not easy to placate his wrath evoked by his father's death, which, of all places, he met in her own chamber. Now, so shortly afterwards, he is to learn of his sister's death. Will not this additional blow throw him back into his former frenzy? Laertes is not given to careful deliberation; his moods are unpredictable; he may act rashly. That is why Gertrude decides to break the bitter news to him herself, and do it in a way that might hurt him as little as possible, and at the same time exonerate her son as much as possible.

These two threads: fear of Laertes and solicitude for Hamlet, condition the veracity of Gertrude's story. In her version Ophelia's action is not suicide, committed in madness, caused by her father's death, who was killed by Hamlet. She tries very artfully to break that chain of causality—and she succeeds: according to her, the poor girl lost her life by mere chance, in an accident that might just as well have happened to a mentally sound person. Oh no—not the slightest connection between her death, her father's death, and Hamlet! Instead of the simple statement: "She went into the water," Laertes is given a colourful picture: the willow—the hoary leaves—fantastic garlands—nettles—daisies—coronet weeds—snatches of old tunes—and all these fantastic ornaments have no other purpose than to divert Laertes's attention from the one fact: through Hamlet he has lost his father—through Hamlet he has now lost his sister also.

Gertrude a fool? A person should be called very shrewd indeed who is capable of handling a situation as delicate as that in so sagacious and persuasive a manner. Nor is this the only occasion where she proves her metal. She shows a similar efficiency in the preceding scene IV. 5, when Laertes, sword in hand, storms into the room: it is evident that without hesitation she steps in between him and Claudius. That is usually interpreted first as a proof of her courage (which she certainly has) and then of her love for her husband. It seems to me, however, that her shielding him is merely an act of self-protection. After all, she has now for better, for worse (more for the worse than the better) linked her own fate with that of Claudius. If she ceases to be his wife she is lost. Should Laertes kill the King, he would not hesitate to kill Hamlet also, at whose hands Polonius died—and where, then, would she be? Of all that she is aware almost instinctively; and, intrepid as she certainly is, she at once steps forward to protect her husband and, with him, herself. She acts with a measure of courage that undoubtedly justifies her description as the "imperial jointress of this warlike state".

*

III

Gertrude's Share in the Crime

THE answer to the question whether Gertrude is a stupid
or a clever woman must have its effect on the still more
important question what the nature of her own crime is
and whether (and if so, to what extent) she is implicated
in the crime committed by Claudius: in her husband's
murder. First, however, it seems to be worth while to
find out how she behaves towards Claudius; for it is clear
that from her outward behaviour deductions can be
drawn as to her inner relation to him.

To begin with, there is a strange disparity between them.
He is always talkative; always eager to have her assent;
he calls her: "My dear Gertrude—sweet Gertrude—sweet
queen", sugaring the honey of his suave solicitude.
Throughout one has the feeling as though he were constantly endeavouring to assuage something in her.

She on the other hand keeps a sullen, almost obstinate
silence. She never talks to him on her own initiative; she
never turns to him for any conversation. She addresses
her son, she speaks to Rosencrantz and Guildenstern, to
Polonius, to Ophelia, to Laertes; but to Claudius she
hardly ever speaks unless she is spoken to and has to
answer.

There are altogether not more than five passages in
which Gertrude addresses her husband. In III. 1. 30 ff
Claudius asks her to withdraw and she answers: "I shall
obey you." In III. 2. 278, when he interrupts the performance of the Mouse-trap and hurries off, she exclaims:
"How fares my lord?" In IV. 1. 5, when he inquires after
Hamlet, she begins her report with the words: "Ah, my
good lord (Q. 2: "Ah, mine own lord") what have I seen
to-night!" In IV. 5. 36, referring to the mad Ophelia, she
says: "Alas, look here, my lord." Finally, in V. 2. 302,

when he warns her not to drink she replies: "I will, my lord; I pray you, pardon me." Throughout she uses invariably the most formal address: "my lord," even when, as in the single case of IV. 1, there is no one else present.

Another strange feature is the fact that, when talking to Claudius, she never makes use of the intimate "thou". When addressing Hamlet she is wont to say "thou" to him. Only at the beginning of the Closet-scene, when he treats her rudely and she feels she must stress her authority, she changes for a while to "you"; and again so when he is in communication with the Ghost and thus alienates himself from her. Yet not even once does she say "thou" to Claudius. Nor does he ever say "thou" to her. That appears all the more remarkable if we remember how Macbeth and his Lady behave and talk to each other: they frequently use the intimate "thou". They are a real couple, sharing love as well as crime. But Claudius and Gertrude? Their crime does not unite them; it separates them like a wall: an invisible, and yet impenetrable wall.

In fact, Gertrude gives the impression of being completely alone. She has no one to whom she could talk in order to relieve her over-burdened heart. Thus it is that the only occasion when she can give expression to her grief is the few moments, in IV. 5. 17 ff, when Horatio leaves her to fetch the distracted Ophelia. There Gertrude has a brief soliloquy:

> "To my sick soul, as sin's true nature is,
> "Each toy seems prologue to some great amiss;
> "So full of artless jealousy is guilt,
> "It spills itself in fearing to be spilt.

Four lines only; but the fact that they are rhymed is certainly no mere chance. (In order to stress their significance the Quarto 2 puts inverted commas in front of each line.)

25

At a similar crossroads Lady Macbeth too has a monologue, also rhymed and also only four lines. She sends
for her husband, at the beginning of III. 2, and before he
comes she speaks to herself:

> Nought's had, all's spent,
> Where our desire is got without content:
> 'Tis safer to be that which we destroy
> Than by destruction dwell in doubtful joy.

These are her only words of self-revelation—and the same
is to be said of Gertrude's soliloquy. At no other time
does she allow us a glimpse of her inner self. A solitary
figure, silent, withdrawing herself from any other contact:
the disconsolate keeper of a nameless secret. Truly, as she
says, her soul is sick.

If we, then, consider Gertrude's behaviour towards her
husband: how she never really speaks to him, how she
never has a question to ask him, never gives him a single
good word—there is one conclusion only: what she feels
for him may be anything; but it certainly is not love.
Once of course it must have been different, or she would
not have been unfaithful to her king. Since then, however,
her relation to him must have completely changed. What
may have caused that emotional eclipse?

There are various questions, considerations, and
suspicions, of which each or several combined may be
relevant.

(a)

It cannot be doubted that Gertrude has committed
adultery. She has done so not merely in the ecclesiastical
sense of the term, i.e., by marrying a brother-in-law (for
that aspect of the matter Shakespeare uses the word
"incest") but adultery in the usual sense. Now, is it
possible to believe that she should not have been startled

by the old King's sudden death? It is common enough amongst adulterers to complain of the obstacle that blocks their path to happiness. And now, when all at once the way is cleared so conveniently, is it reasonable to assume that Gertrude should never have asked a question? Everybody else might have been expected to believe in the story of "the serpent's sting", as indeed they did, since no one besides the two themselves had any idea of the clandestine relations between Gertrude and Claudius. But this indisputably shrewd woman, the adulteress herself, used to telling lies—could she have accepted that tale?

(b)

Why did they marry so hastily? Now after the King's death they could have continued their secret understanding—at least for a time—with greater ease than before. By postponing their marriage, if for a few months only, they would have satisfied the demands of common decency. It appears that it cannot have been their love as such that induced them to marry in that disgraceful haste. Was it perhaps their anxiety to shorten the dangerous period during which an accusation could have been levelled against Claudius? A king, once enthroned and crowned, cannot be brought before the law-courts. And of course the easiest and quickest way of making him king was that of marriage.

Should that have been the consideration that lay at the bottom of their haste, then we are almost bound to assume that she was the murderer's accomplice.

(c)

Still, if we assume that Gertrude, when the play begins, has no suspicion of the murder, does not the play itself offer occasions for her to learn the truth?

27

There is the play-within-the-play. In it, as is generally accepted, the royal couple watch the performance first of the Dumb-show and then of *The Murder of Gonzago*. In either of the interludes the allusions are so palpable that Gertrude, sitting through both of them, must be very stupid indeed if she is not able to see what they imply.

There is moreover Claudius's behaviour that must open her eyes. At the very moment when in the play-scene the murder is performed her husband, with all signs of mental anguish, rises and hurries away, breaking off the entertainment and causing a veritable turmoil. Should we not expect Gertrude to ask him, or herself, a few questions? But she asks no question at all. Does she desist from doing so because she knows of the murder?

However, the play-scene has been interpreted in several ways. My contention is that the Dumb-show was—at the Globe Theatre—performed in such a way that neither the King nor the Queen were in a position to see it, and that the allusions in the spoken play were understandable to Claudius only and no one else. I shall have to return to that subject later.

Yet there is still another occasion where Gertrude must have learned that her husband was murdered, provided she did not know that before. In the Closet-scene Hamlet tells her clearly and expressly that his father was killed. Polonius is slain; Gertrude calls it "a rash and bloody deed"; Hamlet retorts:

> A bloody deed, almost as bad, good mother,
> As kill a king, and marry with his brother.

To this she replies with the repetition:

> As kill a king?

(The question mark is the punctuation of the Folio; the Quarto 2 has a full stop. In the Folio, however, a question

28

mark is often used where we should expect an exclamation mark.)

Gertrude does not repeat the second half of that indictment; to that part she has no answer to make. But her silent acceptance of the smaller point shows that she understands one thing: that Hamlet does not make a general observation, but accuses her own person, and accuses her (a) of murder and (b) of incest. She replies: "As kill a king?" Now, the question is: what is the emotional freight of her exclamation? Does it show astonishment or something else? Is it a sign of innocence or of something else?

Bradley is of opinion that Gertrude was not privy to the murder of her husband, either before the deed or after it. He thinks her exclamation: "As kill a king!" to be "evidently genuine".

Sir E. K. Chambers maintains that she knows nothing of her husband's murder. "She was guilty of a sinful love for Claudius, but was not an accomplice in his greater crime." Professor J. Q. Adams is of opinion that "her bewildered astonishment at the accusation of murder" convinces Hamlet of her innocence of that crime.

Granville-Barker says:

In her bewildered horror she can only echo vaguely: "As kill a king!"

—and then he deals with Hamlet again.

Professor Dover Wilson thinks that Gertrude's "perplexed repetition clears her character for us"; and again: "Her astonishment acquits her for us, as most critics have seen."

Dr. G. I. Duthie, in The 'Bad' Quarto of "Hamlet", refers to Dover Wilson's opinion and adds: "I agree: her innocence is quite clear."

The critics, it appears, are all convinced that Gertrude

29

is not involved in the murder.* There are, however, two
or three points that seem to speak against that assumption.

First, Gertrude's words: "As kill a king?" can certainly
be filled with "perplexity" or "bewilderment"; but they
can express other emotions also, among them horror at
being found out. Words are vehicles only; not their
meaning is decisive, but the emotion which the speaker
wishes them to convey. A guilty Gertrude would repeat
those words just as an innocent Gertrude. If she is
innocent, then her exclamation might be paraphrased
like this: "What did he say? 'As kill a king'? What does
he mean?" If guilty, the paraphrase would run differently:
"What did he say? 'As kill a king'? For heaven's sake,
has he found it out?"

Secondly, what is the effect of Hamlet's words? If
what he says is completely new to his mother, as the critics
assume, what change does it bring about in her attitude
towards Claudius? None at all. Yet if she is innocent,
surely we should expect her to tax her husband with what
she has heard? Would she not report to him, if only as a
warning, what monstrous allegation her son has made?
Yet she does not say a single word. Can it be that this is
so because the "revelation" was no revelation to her?

Finally, what is it that Hamlet speaks about? The
critics seem to assume that he refers to Claudius as
having killed his brother. Yet Hamlet does not speak of
Claudius having killed, but of Gertrude having killed.

A bloody deed, almost as bad, good mother,
As kill a king, and marry with his brother.

The second line cannot have two subjects: "kill a king",
having Claudius as subject, and "marry with his brother",
having Gertrude as subject. Were Claudius the subject
of both parts of the sentence, it would have to read: "As
kill a king, and marry with his widow."

* See Appendix, Note C.

30

This consideration shows that Hamlet accuses his mother (as said before) not only of incest, but also of murder. And when she replies with that repetition: "As kill a king?" he sticks to it:

Ay, lady, 'twas my word.

*

In Quarto 1 the analogous passage contains the same allegation:

> *Ham.* Not so much harme, good mother,
> As to kill a king, and marry with his brother.
> *Queene.* How! kill a king!
> *Ham.* I a King: nay sit you downe. . . .

*

It is a clear and unambiguous accusation; a dreadful indictment. How does Gertrude react to it? She keeps silent. Not a single word comes from her lips. And Hamlet turns back to the dead Polonius:

Thou wretched, rash-intruding fool, farewell.

At so decisive a point, what Gertrude omits to say seems almost more important than what she says.

(d)

Finally there are the four lines, already mentioned, Gertrude's only passage of self-revelation. They occur in IV. 5, i.e., after the Closet-scene.

To my sick soul, as sin's true nature is,
Each toy seems prologue to some great amiss:

31

So full of artless jealousy is guilt,
It spills itself in fearing to be spilt.

The meaning of the lines seems to be this:

"My soul, as the natural result of my sin, is so sick that the smallest trifle seems to me to forebode a disaster. Guilt is so full of irrepressible misgiving that, while dreading to be found out, it betrays itself."*

Were we to find such a deliberation early in the play we should feel inclined to associate it with Gertrude's adultery, despite the fact that even then her fear of being found out or of her guilt betraying itself would appear rather pointless and belated; for meanwhile she has married the adulterer. Yet in iv. 5, what can she mean when she talks of "guilt"? Her own words give a picture of grievous disaster. She speaks of restless fear; she cannot suppress her continuous alarm; she is afraid that her guilt might "spill itself". What does her guilt consist in?

Her adultery is a thing of the past and has not extended into the present. Hamlet has reviled her for her adultery and she has not denied that part of his accusation. That, therefore, has been found out and she need not fear any new discovery on that account. But if we exclude the matter of adultery, as I think we must, what can it be? Is not the only possible answer that what she tries to keep secret is her share in the murder?

*

Dr. Bradley, speaking of Gertrude, says: "She becomes miserable:

To her sick soul, as sin's true nature is,
Each toy seems prologue to some great amiss."

* *See* Appendix, *Note D*.

32

The remaining two lines he omits to quote; throughout his essay he never mentions them.

Sir E. K. Chambers, referring to the four lines, merely says: "Gertrude is still weakly remorseful."

Granville-Barker speaks of Gertrude's assent to see Ophelia and goes on:

. . . and her misery finds vent and relief in the plaintive sing-song of

> To my sick soul, as sin's true nature is,
> Each toy seems prologue to some great amiss:
> So full of artless jealousy is guilt,
> It spills itself in fearing to be spilt.

Then she pulls herself together to receive Ophelia.

That is all. One wonders whether "plaintive sing-song" is an adequate description of that soliloquy and whether Gertrude obtains much "relief" from it. In his separate chapter on Gertrude—among his "Characters"—he does not mention the four lines at all.

In Dover Wilson's *What Happens in "Hamlet"* Gertrude's monologue is not once referred to; it is neither quoted nor dealt with: an astonishing omission.

*

It is the Gertrude of Quarto 2 and First Folio whose character and behaviour have been examined, so far without any definite answer to the question whether she was implicated in her husband's murder or not. What on that point can be said of the other Gertrudes, that of Shakespeare's source and those of later date?

(1) In Belleforest's *Histoires Tragiques* the Queen (Geruthe) does not deny her knowledge of the murder; she merely denies that she ever consented to it: she swears

33

that she would have saved her husband's life had she had
the power to do so.

(2) In *Der Bestrafte Brudermord* the Queen accuses
herself of being the cause of Hamlet's madness. She says:
"Alas! I am very guilty! Had I not married my brother-
in-law, my former husband's brother, I had not done my
son out of the Crown of Denmark!"

(3) In M. Ducis' adaptation, mentioned before, Gertrude
speaks openly of her share in the murder; she wishes
Hamlet to succeed to the throne; and in the end she stabs
herself.

(4) The first performance of *Hamlet* in the German
tongue was that at the Burgtheater in Vienna, on
January 16th, 1773. The text was based on Wieland's
prose translation, the only one then available, published
in 1767. It had for the performance been adapted by
Franz Heufeld, a playwright, who for eight years was
Director of the Burgtheater. The changes he brought
about consisted mainly in cuts (he omitted the Graveyard-scene, combined Rosencrantz and Guildenstern into
one person, etc.) and it is only the end of the play that
was definitely altered.

When Hamlet at the end of the Closet-scene exit,
"tugging in Polonius", Gertrude has a short soliloquy:

> O heaven, where am I? O, woe is me! O earth, open thy
> mouth so that my infamy may be buried there for ever!
> God, what will become of me? (*Exit.*)

In the next scene Claudius decides to send Hamlet to
England; before giving his orders, however, he persuades
the Queen to have "a few minutes of balmy sleep", to
which considerateness she replies:

> To sleep—so sleep——! Shall I ever again be able to
> sleep? Yet it is your wish to be alone, so I go. (*Exit.*)

34

That sounds as if it came from Lady Macbeth rather than from Gertrude. It has obviously been inserted to show her stricken conscience, and also to prepare the audience for the last scene.

In this, Hamlet kills the King, but is immediately threatened by some of the Danes, who, with rapiers drawn, want to avenge their sovereign. Here now the Queen, already on the point of death, gathers her remaining strength and cries:

> Hold, hold, ye Danes! Hear me, hear your dying Queen! In death there is truth. Your King was a murderer; he poisoned my husband; and this your Queen—oh, that my own tongue should accuse me!—I consented to the murder.
> (Thunder. She sinks into a chair. All present start back in astonishment.)

Ham.: Heaven itself confirms her words.

Ger.: O how dreadful, how threatening is the judgement over me! Hamlet, forgive me! Embrace me, once only, Hamlet!

Ham.: Mother, reconcile your soul with heaven!

Ger.: O my son! my crime has robbed me of your heart. O how grimly my vice rages within me, more grimly than the poison! Forgive me, Hamlet; forgive me, ye Danes! Do not let me carry your curse with me to my grave! Your King is avenged! Hamlet, my son—God have mercy upon my soul!

> (She stretches her arms towards Hamlet, but collapses the moment he bends towards her.)

Ham.: O my mother!—God, she is gone. Ill-starred queen! may heaven redeem me from the guilt of your death: (pointing towards the King:) there—there lies your murderer! (To those present:) You who stand around, pale-faced and filled with amazement, trembling

35

at what has happened, you shall be judges between me
and Denmark as to this horrible event: for in your hands
I lay my honour and my justification.
(The end of the tragedy.)

This alteration, with the surviving Hamlet and the
remorsefully confessing Queen, was adopted by Friedrich
Ludwig Schröder at Hamburg in 1776. In the following
year the version was given at Berlin, and later spread all
over Germany. In fact, it held the stage for about fifty
years, until in the 1820s Schlegel's translation succeeded
in replacing that adaptation.

It is characteristic of that age of Enlightenment that
both Ducis and Heufeld deemed it necessary to bring about
an equation between guilt and punishment. Gertrude had
to die, there was no getting round that. On the other
hand those moralizing haberdashers, who were wont to
measure their wares by the yard, did not see why Hamlet,
having committed no crime, should not live and be happy
ever after. And if Gertrude had to pay no less than the
ultimate penalty then her crime must be made a capital
one. To have in the end a dead Gertrude lying about,
without an adequate cause for her death, would have been
indefensible in the eyes of those dealers in justice.

Shakespeare himself never lacks justice; but his justice
is a wholesale one; he does not give change in small coin.
Or, to use another image: his tool is the scythe, not a pair
of scissors.*

*

* David Garrick, too, gave the play with an end of his own making.
There was no voyage to England, no grave-yard scene, no fencing-
match. The Queen escapes alive. "I had sworn," Garrick wrote in a
letter, dated January 10th, 1776, "I would not leave the stage till I had
rescued that noble play from all the rubbish of the fifth act."

Belleforest's Queen Geruthe is psychologically in a position which is virtually the same as that of Queen Gertrude. It would not be possible to identify Shakespeare's Gertrude with the "enlightened" Gertrudes; but, as far as her guilt and conscience go, we might put Belleforest's Queen into Shakespeare's play and not notice any difference. Our Hamlet's mother, too, might have known of the murder before it was committed, herself unable to prevent it (on account of her adultery) or she might have learned of it afterwards. Neither version would, I submit, clash with the text as we have it in Quarto 2 and First Folio.

*

It remains to deal with yet another text, that of Quarto 1. Its interest for the present exposition lies in certain additions to the part of Gertrude. These diverge from the other two texts in such a way that I feel they cannot have sprung from Shakespeare's mind. The passages in question are the following, both of which occur in the Closet-scene.

When the Ghost has left, Gertrude says:

> Alas, it is the weakenesse of thy braine,
> Which makes thy tongue to blazon thy hearts griefe:
> But as I haue a soule, I sweare by heauen,
> I neuer knew of this most horride murder:

A few lines later the two have the following dialogue:

> And mother, but assist me in reuenge,
> And in his death your infamy shall die.
>   *Queene:* Hamlet, I vow by that maiesty,
> That knowes our thoughts, and lookes into our hearts,
> I will conceale, consent, and doe my best,
> What stratagem soe're thou shalt deuise.

37

There are many opinions as to how the text of the Quarto 1 may have come into existence. One school thinks it is a kind of Ur-Hamlet, merely a first draft, yet written by Shakespeare himself. Others attribute it either wholly or partly to Thomas Kyd. Others again think the text to be the original one, but pirated presumably with the help of an actor, who may have played the part of Marcellus or Lucianus, or both. Others take recourse to the assumption of stenography, employed during performances. And the latest suggestion, put forward by Dr. Duthie, is that Quarto 1 post-dates the texts both of Quarto 2 and First Folio, being a memorial reconstruction made by an actor who, where his memory failed him, was able to write blank verse of his own.

Whichever suggestion one is inclined to follow, one thing seems certain: that those additions to the psychological make-up of the play cannot have come from Shakespeare. There are four new points: (a) Gertrude affirms that so far she "never knew" of the murder; (b) she acknowledges that it was murder; (c) Hamlet asks her to assist him in his revenge, promising forgiveness afterwards; and (d) Gertrude assures him of her help in whatever he should devise.

Had it been Shakespeare who made these points, he would have been compelled to re-write the rest of the play. To begin with, Gertrude's attitude towards Claudius would have been fundamentally changed; either she would have openly defied him or been forced into dissimulating her feelings (while showing them to the audience, of course). She would have joined her son in some plot against her husband, or would have had to explain to Hamlet why she could not do what she had promised. She would have prevented his being sent to England or at least would have spoken against it. In the Graveyard-scene she would have taken his part, not sided against him. Finally, she would have acted in a completely different way in the concluding scene, where their secret complicity would certainly have come into the open. Yet of all that we do not see anything. That strange insertion, which comes from nowhere and leads to nowhere, is an erratic block, the product and residuum of an obviously extraneous mentality.

*

In conclusion, neither in the text of Quarto 1 nor in those of Quarto 2 and First Folio does Gertrude's behaviour after the Closet-scene show any change despite the indictment: "As kill a king . . . Ay, lady 'twas my word." The negativeness of her reaction seems to indicate that Hamlet's words have not revealed anything to her beyond what she had known even before the play began.

And that takes us back to that previous occasion on which Gertrude, had she indéed known nothing of the murder, must have been startled and inevitably pushed towards the question why her husband interrupted the performance and fled from the room just at the moment when that ominous murder was enacted.

*

39

IV

The Dumb-Show and "The Murder of Gonzago"

THE poet Karl Immermann, who from 1832–37 was Director of the Stadttheater at Düsseldorf, describes in his "Theater-diarium" his own production of *Hamlet*, and there we find the following passage:

> While the Dumb-show is in progress the King and Queen are chatting, the usual thing among members of the aristocracy. Thus the two conscience-stricken people are yet unaware of what is in store for them. They become attentive only when the spoken play begins.

In England it was J. O. Halliwell-Phillips who, in his edition of the play, 1865, was the first to put the tentative question:

> Is it allowable to direct that the King and Queen should be whispering confidentially to each other during the dumb-show, and so escape a sight of it?

Professor Dover Wilson adopts Halliwell's suggestion and puts all his customary force behind it. He assures us that Claudius does not watch the mimic performance; he maintains that the King as long as the Dumb-show lasts is engaged in a talk with Polonius and the Queen. All the other critics, however, are agreed that Claudius sees and watches first the Dumb-show and then the spoken play. Their opinion can best be summarized in what Granville-Barker says: that a prolonged struggle is going on between the two antagonists in which Hamlet, endeavouring to wear the King down, uses both the Dumb-show and the play; Claudius is strong enough to outface the preliminary

40

ordeal of the Dumb-show, but breaks down in the play itself.

This theory seems, first of all, to be contrary to the old Roman rule: "ne bis in idem," meaning, never to proceed twice in one and the same case. Why should Shakespeare have made use of two instruments to achieve one result if the same result could have been achieved by one instrument? There is such a thing as stage-economy, and the man who wrote *Hamlet* may be trusted to have learned his business by now. There is no reason why he should not have made Claudius break down during the Dumb-show alone, or during the Play-scene alone, if he wanted him to do so. But since he chose to apply a double-instrument he must have pursued a double-purpose.

There is yet another consideration that speaks against the assumption of a double-test, namely that the two instruments, if applied one after the other, have no cumulative effect.. On the contrary: the Dumb-show either gives away the whole stratagem or, at least, must act as a plain warning to Claudius and thus prepare him for the embarrassing implications of the spoken play.

Granville-Barker takes the lines spoken by Lucianus to be "the culmination of a long, tense, deliberate struggle ' between Claudius and Hamlet. But if Shakespeare wishes to have the King forced into an involuntary and irrepressible action of self-betrayal, surely the most effective means would be to spring on him a sudden and completely unforeseen surprise? The whole plan would be in danger of not coming off were Claudius given a warning that would enable him to compose and fortify himself. It is that incongruousness between aims and means that induced Immermann, Halliwell-Phillips, and Dover Wilson to advance their theory that Claudius misses the Dumb-show because he is chatting.

Such an expedient, however, a mere stage trick, is un-Shakespearian. In no other play do we find a parallel to that procedure, namely that it should be left to the actors to cover up an important point of the action by putting their heads together and pretending to have a whispered conversation so that they may prevent themselves from seeing and hearing what is going on around them. Certainly that is not Shakespeare's way, whose wont it is to use "words, words, words".

*

The stage of the Globe Theatre had a balcony. Up on that balcony lies the explanation of many a Shakespearian difficulty and, to my mind, also of that of the Dumbshow.

Of course that balcony was not there for decorative purposes, but was made use of freely and frequently. We may assume that as a rule the shorter scenes and especially those with a few actors only (from two to five or six) were performed on the balcony, the main scenes on the lower stage. We may further assume that in principle the two stages were used alternately: between two scenes on the lower stage there should be one up on the balcony.

That was done, first of all, to add variety to the sequence of the scenes. He would be a poor and unimaginative producer indeed who, having a two-level stage at his disposal, would not make use of it to the full. Yet another reason for employing the upper stage is that a scene performed there "neutralizes" the lower stage, and vice versa. While the action proceeds on the balcony the main stage down below becomes "no man's land", with the result that whoever enters there later carries with him his own time as well as locality. Meanwhile the balcony becomes "no man's land", and so forth in turn. When, e.g., Lady Macbeth in I. 5, letter in hand, appeared —and I have no doubt she appeared on the balcony—she neutralized the stage below, which a moment before was

42

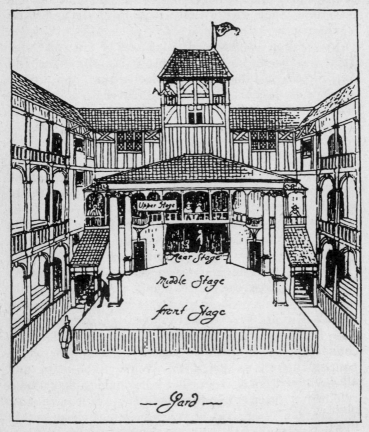

The illustration shows a reconstruction, made by W. H. Godfrey, of the interior of the Fortune Theatre, according to the builder's contract, which has been preserved. The theatre was erected by Peter Street, who only recently had built the Globe Theatre. From the stipulation in the contract that the stage should be "Contryved and fashioned like unto the Stadge of the Plaie house Called the Globe" we may deduce that the general structure of the two stages was more or less identical.

43

a place near the battlefield of Forres and now becomes
Inverness when, the balcony scene over, King Duncan
re-enters.

In addition to the alternating use of the two stages
there was also the possibility of using them simultaneously.
In *Macbeth*, I. 3, the Witches, I feel certain, appeared on
the balcony speaking from there to Macbeth and Banquo
who stood below. Not only would that have been the
most effective but also the easiest way, for the hags to
emerge from behind the balcony curtains and to disappear
by the same means most swiftly. In *Romeo and Juliet*,
I. I, when the fight between the two hostile houses is
going on down below, Prince Escalus addresses his
rebellious subjects from the upper stage. In *Othello*,
II. 3, when down below Montano and Cassio are having
their brawl, the Moor most certainly appeared on the
balcony (where he is presently joined by Desdemona,
"raised up" from her bed) and from the balcony shouted
at them: "What is the matter here?"

In that use to which the two levels of its structure
could be put lies the chief advantage the Elizabethan stage
had over the modern theatre. The possibilities thus
afforded had of course their influence on the plays, their
contents as well as their form. Some of the plays were
obviously written with an eye to the double-stage; others,
originally written for the one-level stage (and such plays
can be found among Shakespeare's also) had to be
refashioned to comply with the demands of the two-level
technique. (That may in some cases have been the
reason why Shakespeare was asked to re-write others'
plays. A close investigation into that question may well
repay the effort.)

To return to *Hamlet*, however. I feel little doubt that
the scene I. 3, between Ophelia, Laertes and Polonius,
was placed on the upper stage. Also the last scene of
Act I was, I should think, performed there. The scene is

44

made up first of two persons, the Ghost and Hamlet, and later of three: Hamlet, Horatio and Marcellus. When Hamlet requests the two others to swear silence and the Ghost "cries under the stage" (a direction to be found in all three versions of the text alike) it seems ludicrous to assume that the actor who played the Ghost should have crept under the boards of the apron stage and moved there from one spot to another crawling. "Under the stage" simply means: "under the upper stage". The Ghost, having descended to the lower stage, would stand beneath the balcony, i.e., in the inner recess, moving behind the back curtain and concealed by it. Also the scenes IV. 2 and IV. 6 were in all probability performed on the balcony; in either only three persons appear: Hamlet with Rosencrantz and Guildenstern in the one, Horatio with a Servant and a Sailor in the other.

Also the first part of the scene V. 2, between Hamlet and Horatio and later Osric and the "Lord", must have been placed on the upper stage. It would have been impossible to let that scene follow immediately after, and on the same stage as, the Graveyard-scene, with no intermediate scene. On a modern stage we drop the curtain on the burial scene and raise it only when the change of scenery is finished. At the Globe Theatre there were only seven lines between Hamlet's exit ("The cat will mew, and dog will have his day") and his re-entry with Horatio. Had he returned on the same level as before, i.e., on the ground stage, the audience would have taken him to have returned to the grave-yard, and would subsequently have assumed that Osric's invitation, the fencing-match, and all the rest took place among the tombs.

There is yet another consideration: King, Queen, Laertes, the Priest, those who carried the coffin (at least two people, probably four), two or three attendants who are called upon when Hamlet and Laertes come to blows, the grave-diggers with their shovels and pickaxes, bier,

45

ropes and coffin—all that crowd could not possibly have left the stage in a flash in order to enable Hamlet and Horatio to return. The ground would not have been neutralized, but still be the cemetery. The difficulty is overcome, however, when we assume that the two, after those seven lines, re-enter not below, but on the balcony.

Osric joins the two and delivers the King's invitation to the fencing-match. Hamlet replies: "Sir, I will walk here in the hall"—and a short move with his hand, pointing to the lower stage, would indicate that he means to have his walk downstairs. Shortly afterwards the "Lord" repeats the invitation. Does he, too, enter on the balcony? He, I should say, appears on the lower stage and speaks up to Hamlet, who answers him from above. That seems to be indicated by the "Lord's" own words: Osric, he says, "brings back . . . that you attend him (the King) in the hall . . ." and adds: "The king and queen and all are coming down." This "down" evidently shows that the "Lord" is standing on the lower stage and that he invites Hamlet to join the Court there, i.e., to descend from the balcony.

The fencing-match must of course have taken place on the lower stage. If, therefore, Hamlet and Horatio had to descend, there must have been time for them to do so. Surely there is time enough? The stage-direction of the Folio reads:

Enter King, Queene, Laertes, and Lords, with other Attendants with Foyles, and Gauntlets, a Table and Flagons of Wine on it.

That of Quarto 2 is even more elaborate:

A table prepared, Trumpets, Drums, and officers with Cushions, King, Queene, and all the state, Foiles, daggers, and Laertes.

46

While all that bustle is going on: table brought in, wine, the foils, chairs put in position and, if we follow the Quarto, while there is music of "trumpets and drums", there is of course ample time for Hamlet to come downstairs and to enter below, to be greeted by Claudius:

Come, Hamlet, come, and take this hand from me.

*

So far I have tried to show that the two-level possibilities of the Globe Theatre were made use of in performances of *Hamlet* as in others. Returning now to the main theme of this chapter, my contention is that (*a*) the Dumb-show was performed on the balcony and (*b*) that *The Murder of Gonzago* was played on the lower stage.

There were four main considerations upon which Shakespeare had to mould his scheme:

(1) He had to inform his audience that what they were going to see, *The Murder of Gonzago*, was meant to show an exact replica of the actual murder of old King Hamlet. Why did he want them to know that beforehand? Because only then could he expect them to concentrate their attention less on the enactment itself than its effect on the King.

(2) At the same time Shakespeare was compelled to find means to prevent the King—and with him the Queen and the courtiers—from seeing the Dumb-show: or else he would have given a warning to Claudius (and in the outcome would have exposed the King's deed to the eyes of the whole Court).

(3) The enactment of the actual murder must have been arranged in such a manner that it did not come as the final climax of a protracted struggle, but as an unexpected blow: or else there would have been the danger of Claudius being able to suppress any sign of self-betrayal.

47

(4) The whole stratagem must have been such that Hamlet did not disobey his father's injunction, namely not to contrive anything against his mother. She, therefore, must have been spared any accusation of complicity in the murder.

All those points are complied with in the case of my suggestion being accepted. I propose to give now a straightforward description of how I consider the two plays, the dumb one and the spoken one, were staged at the Globe Theatre.

*

Lower stage. Flourish. Danish March.

The King and Queen enter, followed by the others: by Ophelia, Polonius, Rosencrantz and Guildenstern; according to the Folio there are "Lords attendant" and also the King's "Guard carrying Torches". They all sit and stand beneath the balcony, facing the audience. The royal couple expect the theatrical entertainment to be performed in front of them, in the centre of the apron stage.

Gertrude invites Hamlet to sit by her. He refuses: "No, good mother; here's metal more attractive." With that he takes Ophelia and, fetching a chair, seats her apart from the others—probably with her back to one of the pillars that support the roof of the balcony. There he sits down himself at her feet. Horatio takes his stand at the other pillar, leaning against it. Thus the three, with their backs to the audience, are in a position to front the King (most important for Hamlet and Horatio, who are to watch his face) and also to look up to the upper stage, while the Court, placed beneath the balcony, are prevented from doing so.

When all are seated Hamlet gives the cue for the beginning, shouting up to the balcony: "for O, for O, the hobby-horse is forgot." Here now the musicians, placed there (evidently the same who executed the Danish March) play their "Hautboys", i.e., they perform what elsewhere (as in *A Midsummer-Night's Dream* and in *As You Like It*) is called "still music": a continuous piece of musical entertainment. At the same time the curtains, drawn aside from the centre of the balcony, "discover" a "Banke of Flowers" or, as it is called in Quarto I, "an Arbor". Upon this bank of flowers or in this arbour the Dumb-show takes its course: loving gestures between "King" and "Queen"; he lies down, she goes off. The "Fellow" poisons the "King". The "Queen" returns and makes "passionate action". "Two or three Mutes" come and carry the dead body away. The "Poisoner" re-enters, woos and in the end wins the "Queen". The curtains close again, the music ceases. The Dumb-show is over, and in a moment or two the Prologue will enter—below of course—to announce the beginning of the spoken play.

Now, however, the obvious question is: what are the people on the lower stage doing while the Dumb-show is in progress above? The mimic performance, no matter how swiftly performed, would take three to five minutes. During this time, will not the Court become suspicious that something is going on over their heads? Yet on second thoughts, why should they? They are in the same position as the audience in a modern theatre who find—to their delight or annoyance, it all depends—that first an overture has to be listened to. Claudius and Gertrude know already from the Danish March that up on the balcony there are the musicians; and if these, before the play begins, give a musical introduction, what is there to arouse suspicion?

What, on the other hand, are Hamlet, Ophelia and Laertes doing? They alone, beside the real audience, are in a position to watch the Dumb-show—and they do so: we learn that from the comments Ophelia and Hamlet

49

make on what they are seeing. (From the King's party,
conspicuously enough, there is not a single word.) While
the mimic performance is in actual progress Ophelia
enquires twice: "What means this, my lord?" and:
"Belike this show imports the argument of the play?"
Hamlet replies: ". . . it means mischief" and again: "We
shall know . . . the players . . . tell all." Immediately
it is over she again stresses the important point: "Will
they tell us what this show meant?" and once more Hamlet
reassures her: "Ay." In this most ingenious way we learn
from Ophelia, who acts as Presenter, that the mimic
performance is "the argument" of the play that is to
follow. This, we understand, will contain nothing new,
but be a mere repetition in words of what we have seen
in the mummery.

Still, the technical objection may be raised as to
whether those six or eight lines between Hamlet and
Ophelia are not heard by the King and the others: if this
were so their attention would be drawn to the balcony.
Yet there is first the fact that the two are sitting some
distance away from the royal party; then, that they are
supposed to be speaking intimately, he sitting at her
feet, and finally that, according to stage convention, their
conversation is "drowned" in the accompanying music,
while to the real audience their words should of course be
perfectly audible. (The question whether Hamlet's
indecent remarks are meant to be overheard by the whole
Court or addressed to Ophelia alone is certainly of consequence both to his character and the nature of the
relation between himself and Ophelia.)

*

Thus, by placing the Dumb-show on the upper stage
and making Ophelia act as Presenter, Shakespeare
achieves two of his aims: first, he informs his audience

that the spoken play will merely repeat the mimed play and, second, he prevents the King and his people from seeing the mimic part altogether. Claudius, so far, has not the slightest forewarning why he should be wary of what is to follow that musical introduction.

At the same time, however, the audience have been put in much the same position as that in which Hamlet stands: they also know now in advance the contents of *The Murder of Gonzago*. Hamlet has told Horatio:

> There is a play to-night before the king;
> Once scene of it comes near the circumstance
> Which I have told thee of my father's death . . .

and he has asked him to observe his uncle:

> . . . give him heedful note:
> For I mine eyes will rivet to his face. . . .

This is essentially what Shakespeare asks of his own audience: "Rivet your eyes on Claudius's face." And they will certainly do so; for now they know: in that silent war between Hamlet and his uncle the battlefield is now indeed Claudius's face. Will he show any sign of alarm and thus betray himself? In that case the Ghost did speak the truth and Claudius did commit the murder. In that case Hamlet can have no further doubt and will without further delay, so they must assume, do everything to achieve his revenge.

There is, however, one consideration: what if Claudius smells a rat and, crime-hardened as he is, concentrates all his power of self-command in order to suppress his alarm? This, it is evident, is Shakespeare's particular concern. What he needs, to counteract that danger of self-command, was not a protracted struggle, but an irresistible sudden blow, coming down like a flash of lightning from the blue sky. To administer that blow Shakespeare makes use of two things: (*a*) he chooses a kind of murder as conspicuous and peculiar as possible, and (*b*) he saves up and accumulates all the means of surprise for the one decisive moment: that in which the murder itself is enacted.

Looking at it from that angle we understand why Shakespeare should have chosen a type of murder so strange and out of the way as pouring poison into a sleeper's ear. This method of killing is so conspicuous that it sticks in the mind, lends itself most easily to be enacted by mummery, and is, above all, so singular that the murderer, confronted with the image of that kind of murder, cannot possibly say: "Ah, so many murders have been committed: why should this enactment represent my own deed?" A poisoned cup, or a stab in the back, or strangling, or any other of the usual ways of killing would have been unsuspicious; but seeing enacted so abnormal and peculiar a murder as killing through the ear, the culprit cannot possibly help recognizing: "That means myself." No other conclusion but that his crime has been discovered.

Still, for a hard-bitten criminal to realize that he has been found out does not yet mean that he must betray himself.* Shakespeare had to make sure that the whole and concentrated force of surprise burst on the King. What has he done to achieve that?

He has, I should say, done everything the situation offers to hold back the surprise until the very last moment. Here now the reader will be surprised at the absence of certain features in the spoken play, just as I myself was surprised when I first looked for them, and looked in vain. To my astonishment I noticed that two things are absent from the text: (1) any indication or

* Prof. J. Q. Adams maintains that Claudius "suppresses his emotions by an effort of the will".

allusion that the two speakers are "King" and "Queen", and (2) anything to show that they are in a "garden".

The husband who talks to his wife of their thirty years' married life addresses her as "love" and "sweet", but never as "sweet queen" or anything that might indicate her royal position. She addresses him as "my lord" and speaks of "my husband", but never alludes to his being king. He speaks of himself as "thy first lord"; she promises that, should she become a widow, she would never be "wife" again. Nor is there, in that very long dialogue, any allusion to kingdom, realm, throne, crown or sceptre; nothing is said about succession or about an heir, things that usually haunt the mind of a king who is worried about his imminent death. For all we hear from them, he might be an old silversmith or a retired judge or an astronomer. And they might be in their bedroom. Not a word occurs that would imply "garden". At the end he simply says:

> Sweet, leave me here awhile,
> My spirits grow dull, and fain I would beguile
> The tedious day with sleep.   (*Sleeps.*)

—whereupon she replies:

> Sleep rock thy brain,
> And never come mischance between us twain. (*Exit.*)

Neither of them mentions the "bank of flowers" or "arbour" or anything else that might indicate that they are in the open.

I cannot but assume that the omission of all those indications is not only deliberate, but brought about with very great care. It is all part of the scheme of surprise. And this surprise is all the stronger since, as I feel certain, the couple perform their parts in the spoken play without

53

any regalia, i.e., with no kingly robes and no crowns on their heads.

For between the dumb and the spoken play there is this difference: the former is meant for the real audience and must be as plain and explicit as possible; the latter is meant for the stage audience, for Hamlet's private audience, so to speak, and must be as indistinct as possible. Its meaning must be unrecognizable until the very last moment; and even the implication of the last moment, that of the actual murder, must be recognizable to the King, but to no one else.

On the upper stage we have the "garden", represented by the "bank of flowers" or the "arbour", put there in full sight. There, the "garden" is indispensable, for the Ghost has told us that he was murdered while asleep. (To stress that point Shakespeare makes him speak of the garden twice: "sleeping in mine orchard," I. 5. 35, and: "Sleeping within mine orchard," 59.) To make it clear that the victim is "King" he has, absurd as it is, to carry his crown into the garden for his afternoon nap. To make it still clearer the "Poisoner" lifts up the crown, thus showing it to the whole house, and kisses it. No one should be left with any doubt that what is shown is the reconstruction of the Ghost's story: that he has been

Of life, of crown, of queen, at once dispatched.

When, after the crown, the "Poisoner" has won the "Queen", too, the curtains are drawn again in front of the balcony, and the second part is transferred to the lower stage.

While the Prologue enters ceremoniously, makes his bow, delivers his speech (and perhaps drops a cushion in front of the royal couple) bows once more and retires, there is sufficient time for the two actors, the "King" and the "Queen", to come downstairs and enter below. (In the speech-headings they are still called "King" and "Queen", but that may easily mean the two actors who in the Dumb-show had acted the parts. How else could Shakespeare refer to them since in the spoken play they are meant to remain anonymous?) He, if my suggestion is accepted, appears without his crown, and at the end of their conversation lies down at the feet of Claudius and Gertrude—on the bare ground, laying his head on a cushion that either the Prologue has put there or which the "Queen" considerately provides for his comfort.

When he falls asleep and his wife exit, there had been tactless talk about second marriage, but neither Claudius nor Gertrude nor anybody of the Court have seen or heard the slightest hint that might portend any danger to the sleeping silversmith or, least of all, foreshadow an act of murder. None of them can guess what the real audience know: that there in front of them lies old King Hamlet, meant to be murdered once more, murdered through his ear.

Of course Gertrude is not pleased with the contents of the play so far: she is annoyed, but nothing more. When Hamlet asks her how she liked the play she replies:

The lady protests too much, methinks.

(Significantly she calls her "the lady", and not "the queen", which seems to corroborate that the two characters are not recognizable as being royal.) And when Claudius, he, too, irritated by that second-marriage business, enquires quite innocently whether there is "no offence" in the play, it is left to Hamlet to drop the first ominous word: "they do but jest", he explains, "poison in jest . . . the image of a murder done in Vienna. . . ." At this Claudius may prick up his ears; but by now it is too late: there already is Lucianus, approaching his victim.

Does he hold up the vial? Perhaps; perhaps not. Even

55

if he does there is still no cause for Claudius to suspect
that the image of a murder done in Vienna could be an
image of his own crime. Why indeed should he have any
suspicion of its having been discovered? Hamlet has never
given any indication that he knows of the murder. How
could he? There was no witness when the deed was done.
And if some murderer in Vienna had a vial of poison and
held it up before he used it, what had that to do with him,
Claudius? Nothing at all. And if Lucianus did not hold
up the poison, the less occasion for Claudius to give even
the slightest thought to his own crime, of which, he is
quite sure, no one has the slightest idea.

And now Lucianus speaks. He speaks of "drugs fit",
of "mixture rank", of "Hecate's ban". Still nothing to be
really alarmed at. But then—he lifts up the poison—
and pours it into the sleeper's ear——!

That is unmistakable. Now there can be no doubt:
Hamlet knows all.

The King rises. The play is over. The Mouse-trap has
done its work.

*

Thus, by making use of the double-stage, Shakespeare
achieves everything. The real audience know that the
king who had just appeared in the Dumb-show and appears
now again on the lower stage is old Hamlet. They know
that what had happened to him in reality some months
ago and had just been shown on the balcony will now
again be enacted, this time before the murderer's own eyes.
Claudius, on the other hand, is absolutely unprepared.
Thus it is that the blow, eagerly awaited by the audience,
comes down on Claudius like a thunder-clap. His surprise
is so sudden and violent that he is unable to restrain
himself.

There is yet another point, one which it would have

been impossible to achieve without the help of the two-level stage. That is the fact that what is now known between Hamlet and Claudius remains unknown to the Court. Hamlet, after the Mouse-trap, is now sure that Claudius did murder the King, and Claudius knows now that Hamlet knows it. But what about the others?

Bradley put his finger on the sore spot. He wondered why no one among the courtiers, having seen the Mouse-trap, "shows any sign of perceiving in it also an accusation of murder. Surely," he adds, "that is strange."

Yet the problem disappears if my suggestion is accepted. After what, to the King's party, was nothing but a musical overture, the sum total of the theatrical performance, as seen by them, is this: An old man, "so sick of late," talks of death and second marriage. No one recognizes him as a king, still less as old Hamlet. The old King, they know, was stung by a serpent in his garden. In the spoken play there is no garden and the sleeper is murdered in a manner of which they have never heard before. For them, between the death of their old King and this murder scene there is not the slightest resemblance; better to say, this stage murder simply does not remind them of old Hamlet's death.

Were that different it would have been necessary for Shakespeare to re-write the remainder of the play. Had the courtiers seen the Dumb-show, or had they understood that in the spoken play the old man was to be taken for "a king", then Polonius, Rosencrantz and Guildenstern, and in fact the whole Court would have put two and two together. Yet none of them shows any change in his behaviour, no one asks any question: it is evident that no suspicion has been roused.

Not in them. But what about Gertrude? The only person who is at least one step ahead of the others, has she too no question to ask? True, she does not see the Dumb-show any more than do the others. But first she

listens to a husband who prophesies to his wife that after
his death she would marry again. Claudius asks: "Is there
no offence in't?" The murder is enacted. At that, her
husband starts up, evidently filled with horror at what he
has seen. He is the man with whom she had deceived her
first husband. Can we really take it that she is suddenly
struck with blindness, deafness and imbecility?

Still, of one suspicion we have to acquit her: obviously
she does not know the manner in which old Hamlet was
killed; or she would, just as Claudius, have recognized
that the Mouse-trap was an enactment of her first husband's murder. In this case she would not only have
shown similar alarm, but would in the Closet-scene have
opened the gambit of her altercation with a different move.
As it is, she wishes to scold her son for nothing but having
"offended" his stepfather. By this she apparently means
Hamlet's tactlessness in making the players speak of
second marriage.

Yet even if we have to acquit her of directly co-operating
in the murder or of knowing exactly how Claudius
committed it, does that mean that we have to acquit her
of complicity altogether?

Perhaps she consented to the murder and Claudius
said to her—in the words of Lady Macbeth—: "Leave all
the rest to me."

Or perhaps she was opposed to his plan, but was
unable to prevent its execution; perhaps he had her
completely in his power and, in view of their adultery,
blackmailed her into acquiescence.

Or perhaps he kept her in ignorance about time,
occasion and manner of the crime and told her, another
Macbeth:

> Be innocent of the knowledge, dearest chuck,
> Till thou applaud the deed.

Whether Gertrude consented freely, or was compelled to keep inactive, or heard of the deed afterwards, we have no means of knowing. Yet there is little doubt in my mind that, when the play begins, she knows of the accomplished fact.

*

Professor E. E. Stoll (in *Shakespeare and Other Masters*) deals with the question, slightly touched upon by Bradley, in which way the Dumb-show and the spoken play effect not only Claudius and Gertrude, but the whole Court. He says:

> And if at the theatrical entertainment he (Claudius) is clever enough, but grits his teeth and braces himself, what of the whole Court there that never takes the hint? What of the Queen both here and in the Closet-scene? In every story there must be an obstacle, and in many of the greatest . . . it is here or there rather arbitrary or improbable. There is no more psychology, or even simple motivation, underlying the lack of effect on the Court than there is, for that matter, in the expectation of any effect upon the criminal in the first place. . . .

This denial of any psychology in the set-up of the Mouse-trap, even of any "simple motivation" in it, seems to do little justice to Shakespeare's craftsmanship.

*

V

"SOMETHING . . .
OF HAMLET'S TRANSFORMATION . . ."

So far, little has been said of Hamlet himself. That does
not seem unnatural in an enquiry primarily concerned
with his father. The Ghost, though not the protagonist,
is the real motive power of the play. For long stretches
he keeps behind (or under) the stage. Yet all the time—
"seeing, unseen"—he watches the progress of his case and
is prepared to intervene if need be. It is his own case that
he pursues through all the vicissitudes, and when his
representative appears to falter, when it seems as if the
great enterprise were not only losing its pith and moment,
but would altogether its "current turn awry", he does not
hesitate to take matters into his own hands again.

What has old Hamlet told his son and required of him?
If we are to sum up, it comes to this: Claudius is an
"incestuous and adulterate beast"; he has "gifts that
have the power to seduce"; he "won to his shameful lust"
the queen who proved to be "seeming-virtuous" only. He,
the father, was murdered by that wretch who now wears
the crown of Denmark.

This, freed from elaboration, is what Hamlet learns
about the crime committed. In the end he is called upon:

> If thou hast nature in thee, bear it not,
> Let not the royal bed of Denmark be
> A couch for luxury and damned incest.

And immediately follows the injunction:

> But howsoever thou pursu'st this act,
> Taint not thy mind; nor let thy soul contrive
> Against thy mother aught; leave her to heaven,

60

And to those thorns that in her bosom lodge
To prick and sting her.

It is two different things that make up old Hamlet's
indictment: (*a*) incestuous adultery and (*b*) murder. It
lies in the nature of the crime that the adultery refers to
both Claudius and Gertrude; the murder, on the other
hand, may have been committed either by Claudius alone
or by both of them. As to his brother the Ghost is quite
clear; he demands of his son (I. 5. 23–25):

If thou didst ever thy dear father love . . .
Revenge his foul and most unnatural murder.

As to Gertrude, however, he is conspicuously indistinct.
True, he does not say that she helped in the murder; but
neither does he say anything to the contrary. His speech
takes some eighty lines; certainly there would have been
space enough to state in a few words that she did not know
of the deed, nor does so now.

Yet such a word would have been highly appropriate,
first of all to quieten the troubled mind of a son who
undoubtedly must tremble at the thought that his own
mother might have consented to her husband's assassination. Should we not expect the Ghost to utter that one
word of relief (the word: "she is innocent") if he could
have done so? Also it is obvious from all we hear that he
still loves Gertrude and is full of considerateness for her.
This being so, would it not be natural for him, if only for
Gertrude's sake, to reassure his son of her innocence?
Would that not save Hamlet from torturing himself as
well as his mother? But we hear nothing of the sort. We
only hear the Ghost speak of "thorns that in her bosom
lodge" and "prick and sting her". The inevitable result is
a smarting doubt in Hamlet's soul: do those "thorns" refer
to the adultery only or to the murder also? That is the
question.

61

However, the Ghost is silent on that point, and we cannot turn his deliberate silence into an open accusation. Yet it is obvious that Hamlet is haunted by that question. He with his shrewd intellect must of course ask himself time and again how and how closely and to what extent the adultery had been connected with the murder. A brain as penetrating as his must be tortured by those suspicions. Up to III. 2 he is yet uncertain whether the Ghost was a good spirit or the devil and whether, therefore, his revelation can be relied upon or not. But that query answered,—and the answer was Claudius's self-betrayal—the far more important question obtrudes itself once more, and this time with tenfold force: How did the adultery lead to the murder? Is his mother guilty of the one crime only or of both?

I have just used the expression: "the more important question"; what I mean is, important to Hamlet. For his father, the question is not important at all: the Ghost knows the answer although he does not speak of it. Yet between him and Hamlet there is this difference: the son wishes to discover the truth; the father wishes to conceal the truth. It is this divergency of interest and purpose that leads to the danger of their ways separating. That is why the Ghost suddenly appears in the Closet-scene.

*

One cannot say that the Ghost, when speaking to Hamlet, tells him a lie; but he does not tell him the truth either, at least not the whole truth. It is this half-truth that creates the twilight under which the play is kept right down to Gertrude's death. At the moment she dies everything seems clear and all problems are solved. It is the Ghost's ambiguity that pushes Hamlet into the darkness in which he gropes for an answer: the answer to a question he does not dare to ask either himself or his mother, for fear lest he should become another Orestes or, to use his own words, lest the soul of Nero should enter his bosom.

We cannot imagine that the Ghost would not have spoken of, and even emphasized, Gertrude's innocence had he been in a position to do so. Unable on the one hand to pronounce her guiltless and avoiding on the other to declare her guilty, he leaves the question (for his son a burning question) unanswered. Thus he lays on Hamlet's soul not only the task of revenge, but also the doubt about his mother's crime.

This doubt is for Hamlet the heavier burden. To avenge his father's death is, as soon as the Ghost's story is confirmed, so to speak a merely technical problem: it involves no psychological difficulty; it only needs to be executed, and that can be done at any convenient time or place. Far more complicated and, for him, far more vital is his desire to discover the truth about his mother's complicity. He could easily kill Claudius when he finds him at prayer. But Hamlet is now so occupied with his self-imposed task as to his mother that for the moment he neglects the task imposed on him by his father. Either way he violates the Ghost's command, and it is for those two reasons that the Ghost finds it necessary to appear in person to set his son right again.

*

When in I. 5 the Ghost disappears ("Hamlet, remember me") it takes some time for his revelation to sink into Hamlet's consciousness. First, there is only one line that refers to his mother:

O most pernicious woman!

—and then he turns to the "smiling villain" again. After

63

that, until the Mouse-trap scene, he neither meets his
mother nor does he speak of her. Yet all the time the
poisonous doubt, instilled by his father's half-silence, goes
on working in his soul: it destroys his faith in womankind.
"Frailty, thy name is woman"; that he had known before
the Ghost had spoken to him. Now he has learned that
woman can be worse than frail, and the acid of that new
perception eats away all his tenderness towards the other
sex. It is not, as Ophelia takes it, his noble mind that is
o'erthrown; it is his "milk of human kindness" that has
been transformed into "cursed Hebona". What the whole
Court notices in him, what they call madness, is in reality
the bitterness of his moral anguish, the agony of his lost
faith in the goodness of woman.

Both Ophelia and Polonius are convinced that in the
silent scene described by her (II. 1) Hamlet's behaviour
was that of a madman. Of course Ophelia cannot understand what is going on in Hamlet's tortured soul; still less
can her father. Hamlet's "transformation" due to his
being jilted by Ophelia? But he is not the man to allow
himself to be jilted. Three monosyllables would regain
him all her love. She did "repel his letters" and "deny his
access to her"? In his state of mind he has certainly
not even noticed that. And in fact, do we not see that he
simply walks into her closet? Of course he cannot tell her
why he has come and what is the reason for his visit; for
in that case he would have had to tell her about his
mother's adultery, and perhaps even more than that.
Thus, whatever his intention, he must keep silent—and she
takes that silence for madness.

What indeed is Hamlet's intention when he breaks
into the quietness of her room? Is it, as Chambers maintains, that he expects her to give him "strength to
accomplish his mission" or "help of spiritual sympathy"?
Or is it, as Dover Wilson suggests, that he seeks her out
"in the hope of finding consolation and help in her

presence"? But she does nothing for him, Dover Wilson
goes on to say: "her face reflects fear alone . . . and so,
after a long pause, waiting for the help that never comes,
he takes his leave." Bradley on the other hand thinks
that Hamlet's appearance and behaviour "are those of a
man crazed with love".

I hesitate to agree with those interpretations. First,
what is the meaning of that strange neglect in his attire?
Hamlet appears

> . . . with his doublet all unbraced,
> No hat upon his head, his stockings fouled,
> Ungarter'd and down-gyved to his ancle . . .

Still, this disordered attire may have been intended—so
Professor Dover Wilson thinks—to denote "antic disposition". But then Ophelia tells us that Hamlet was

> Pale as his shirt, his knees knocking each other,
> And with a look so piteous in purport
> As if he had been loosed out of hell
> To speak of horrors: he comes before me.

In this "sore distraction", Dover Wilson says, Hamlet
"instinctively turns for support to the only being left
who might give it him. She fails; and the 'piteous' sigh
shows that he realizes her failure, and that all is over
between them."

I should have said that a man who is pale as his shirt,
trembling from head to foot and altogether looking as if
coming straight from hell, is either on the point of taking
his own life or has just attempted to do so. With somebody to whose mind that thought is not foreign (the
thought of "self-slaughter", of "To be or not to be") that
surmise is perhaps not too wide of the mark. Still, it is a
surmise only. Thus much, however, seems certain:
Hamlet must have suffered a complete breakdown, and

this—at least so I think—was probably caused by his linking adultery with murder. Brooding over the Ghost's revelation, trying to find the connection between the part of the story he has been told and the part left untold, he must have reached a point where he imagined he had found the truth, i.e., where he felt that his mother must have known of the murder.

This suspicion must have come down on him with the force of a sledge-hammer, crushing all his tender emotions, faith, love—everything. In his youthful rashness and implacability he at once sees in every woman another Gertrude, ready like her to violate every commandment for the sake of her sensual pleasure. At once he rushes into Ophelia's room. He wants nothing from her, neither consolation nor help to accomplish his mission. His only desire is to shout in her face the whole bitterness of his accusation, to splash her with the poison of his misogyny— and remembering how he rages at her in the Nunnery-scene, although by then the fire of his passion has burnt down, we can imagine how he would have railed at her if only he had been free to vent his emotions. But his mouth is sealed—by his father's injunction—and we can well understand his being pale and his trembling if we consider the force he must have needed to suppress an outburst. It is a farewell. She stands for his mother, for woman in general, for that faithless, treacherous sex. Having "perused" her face ("Is it possible: so beautiful, and yet so wicked, so vile, so infernally bad!") he shakes himself free and breaks with her, as he thinks, for ever.

Ophelia describes her visitor's looks and behaviour accurately; but she has not the subtlety either of mind or heart to understand his silence. (Cordelia might have understood him; but then, she was not first and foremost obedient to her father, whereas it is Ophelia's prime fault that she obeys hers too much.) And Polonius would never have understood, even had a flood of words been wasted

66

on him. Hamlet is not, as Polonius mistakes him to be, in "the very ecstasy of love"; it is the very ecstasy of despair, despair of woman.

*

Seen from that point of view the story of Hamlet's visit appears to take on its proper function, which is, to link the Hamlet of the first act with that of the Mouse-trap. In the soliloquy: "O, that this too, too solid flesh would melt . . ." he disapproves of the haste of his mother's second marriage, not of the marriage itself. Had she waited a reasonable time he would have assented to her re-marrying, and also accepted the choice of her husband. What in his mother's behaviour seems to him so loathsome is merely the time factor: that she married "with such dexterity"

After that visit, however, Hamlet's mind seems poisoned. It is as though a drop of that "leperous distil-ment" that curdled his father's blood had entered his brain—as in fact it did: for it is the suspicion dropped by the Ghost, the suspicion about Gertrude's share in the murder, that brings about that psychological revulsion. From now onwards, whenever woman is mentioned Hamlet cannot help—so it seems—uttering, or rather vomiting forth, his loathing for those ambling and lisping wantons that "nickname God's creatures".

In his first appearance after that visit, in the scene (II. 2) with Polonius, it is none other than the word "carrion" that reminds him of Ophelia. Reading in his book he comes across the term: "a good kissing carrion"— and at once he turns to Polonius: "Have you a daughter?" When shortly afterwards Rosencrantz and Guildenstern quite innocently speak of Fortune it is the noble prince who drags in a smutty joke. In fact, expressions such as "strumpet—bawd—whore—drab—scullion" are now

67

frequently used by him. And when in the Play-scene,
talking to Ophelia, he indulges in gross indecencies
(". . . between maid's legs . . . be not you ashamed to
show . . . puppets dallying . . . it would cost you a
groaning . . .") we should not try, as Granville-Barker
does, to find excuses in the "freedom of speech" at
Renaissance Courts or in other whitewash. Hamlet's talk
is foul because the sweet water of his mind has been
befouled. What we hear is his sex-nausea; his mouth is
bitter with it. It is not Ophelia ad personam whom he
wishes to insult, but Ophelia as representing the sex to
which his mother belongs.

From his bitter anguish we may judge his former
feelings for his mother: for only a being whom we love
deeply can hurt us so deeply.

*

68

VI

The Ghost's Hic et Ubique

STILL, so far all Hamlet's suspicions, however strong and however painful and distressing, are mere suspicions. Whether they are to become hard facts or disappear into nothing depends on whether or not the Ghost spoke the truth. To find that out, Hamlet invents the Mouse-trap. In it, however, he intends to catch no one but the King. It would not be necessary to catch his mother also; for should it turn out that the Ghost can be trusted in one aspect, then there is no reason why Hamlet should not accept the whole of the story. Also it would not be feasible to hold both King and Queen in their seats if too much were to be presented before their eyes. If he showed an unfaithful wife the performance would certainly be interrupted before the murder could be shown. Finally there is his father's injunction not to contrive anything against his mother. For all these reasons Hamlet confines himself to setting the trap for Claudius alone.

But then the Play-scene is over. There is no longer any doubt that the Ghost's story is true: Claudius did kill his brother. Now, if it is true that he committed the murder, then it is true that he committed adultery also; and if they committed adultery, then . . . Once more the question looms up, threatening like a gloomy cloud: how far was she involved in the murder?

His mother sends for him. Rosencrantz delivers her message: she desires to speak with him in her closet. He makes the cruel reply:

We shall obey, were she ten times our mother.

And as soon as the others leave him all his suppressed rage breaks forth:

69

> 'Tis now the very witching time of night . . .
>   . . . now could I drink hot blood
> And do such bitter business as the day
> Would quake to look on. Soft now, to my mother . . .

Quarto 2 has: "soft, now to my mother . . .", but I prefer, here as almost always, the punctuation of the Folio, as given above. Modern editors have usually: "Soft! now to my mother . . ." This looks as if Hamlet speaks first of what he is going to do to Claudius, and then turns from him to his mother. Yet "soft" is, as the *Shorter Oxford English Dictionary* puts it, merely "an exclamation with imperative force either to enjoin silence or deprecate haste". The words "soft now" do not indicate a division in Hamlet's thoughts; throughout this soliloquy his mind is with his mother. Were it otherwise, what is the business he speaks of, so bitter that the day "would quake to look on"? Surely to avenge one's father by killing his murderer would be an act of justice and cannot be described in so terrifying terms?

I feel convinced that we have to take the soliloquy as a whole. And if we ask what Hamlet is thinking of, the answer, both simple and frightful, is: matricide. Such an act the world would indeed quake to look on. He could do it, he says, and yet——:

> O heart, lose not thy *nature*; let not ever
> The *soul of Nero* enter this firm bosom:
> Let me be cruel, *not unnatural*;
> I will *speak daggers* to her, but *use none*:
> My tongue and soul in this be hypocrits.
> How in my words soever she be shent,
> To give them *seals*—never, my soul, consent!

He apostrophizes himself to abstain from stabbing his mother. First: "heart, lose not thy nature". It is

70

" 'gainst nature", as the Old Man in *Macbeth* (II. 2) puts it, "to ravin up thine own life's means". To make it still clearer Hamlet refers to Nero, who murdered his own mother, who had poisoned her husband. Daggers would he speak, but "use none". And once more: to give "seals" to his words, i.e., to finish them off with a thrust of his dagger—"never, my soul, consent!"

He is frank enough, as outspoken as one can be if speaking of the most execrable crime in mankind, of which even a completely dehumanized being would speak with awe-struck reticence. Just his outspokenness shows, should any doubt be left, that he never would take his mother's life, however much she might enrage him. And yet, the mere fact that the idea did enter his mind, and that he has to dispute it within himself before he sweeps it away, should make us think.

Taking for granted that Hamlet only speaks of matricide, but would never do the deed, there is still the question: What is the crime that, if ascertained, would justify in a son's mind the infliction on his mother of the death penalty? What has Gertrude done for which Hamlet thinks his mother deserves that punishment? Her adultery has been partly absolved by time and subsequent marriage. Can we assume that his thoughts still dwell on the adultery, just now, immediately after the Mouse-trap has proved that his father was murdered? I think we are forced to take it that he suspects his mother of complicity in the murder: only then does it seem imaginable that so sensitive and gentle a man as Hamlet should ever conceive the idea of matricide.

To clear up the question of his mother's guilt ranks topmost in his mind. Compared with that, everything must take second place, even the revenge on Claudius. He rather sheathes his sword, already drawn: first he must make sure whether, and if so how deeply, she was involved in the murder.

71

This now is the point where he swerves from the path his father wishes him to take. So far, the Ghost has had no reason to intervene: things are developing slowly, but no error has occurred yet. Here and now, however, his son strives to penetrate into a region from which he wishes him to keep away. Gertrude's husband does not wish his son to know the whole truth.

What the Ghost intends is to have his own death avenged on Claudius: at the same time he wishes Gertrude to be spared. He is to die, she to live. This scheme is endangered if Hamlet is suffered to pursue his private inquiry into her guilt. The danger is manifold: Gertrude might confess, Claudius might be warned; Gertrude might kill herself, and Claudius might escape his punishment; Hamlet might become a matricide and thus either forgo his duty of revenge or catastrophically overdo it. The Ghost foresees those possibilities, and intervenes. He does so with a dual purpose: to prevent Hamlet from going too far, and to lead him back to his initial duty.

*

What, on the other hand, is Hamlet's intention in the Closet-scene?

Let us recapitulate that, at the beginning of the scene, he does not only speak openly of his father's murder, but unmistakably taxes his mother with the deed or, at least, with the knowledge of it:

A bloody deed, almost as bad, good mother,
As kill a king, and marry with his brother.

When she replies:

As kill a king?

72

—which may equally import guilt and innocence—he insists:

> Ay, lady, 'twas my word.

There follows the incident with Polonius. Hamlet proceeds to compare the two pictures. Then he goes on to abuse Claudius: "A murderer and a villain"—the word "murderer" comes in now as a matter of course—"a slave . . . a vice of kings . . . a cutpurse . . ."—and one must ask: What is he driving at? What is his aim?

It is the disclosure of Gertrude's share in the murder. Of course he cannot put the direct question: "What was your part in that crime?" By doing so he would only lay open his ignorance and merely invite her to shirk the answer or to deny all knowledge of it. He therefore takes the line of pretending to know what there is to be known, waiting for her either to affirm it or at least not to deny it. He has spoken of "killing the king" and here, speaking of Claudius, he openly uses the term: "murderer". He has already shaken her self-composure, and now he is on the point of breaking it down altogether. Their speeches are now simultaneous. (Which is shown by the fact that his lines, although appearing to the eye as broken-off, continue in one flow, not interrupted by her interjections.) He shouts at her, she sobs. Her resistance is already reduced to a helpless: "no more, sweet Hamlet . . . no more . . ." Were he permitted to continue his railing, Gertrude, dissolved in tears, would give up all resistance—and confess. It is at this crucial point and in order to prevent that confession that old Hamlet appears and thus interrupts them.

*

Other critics have taken a different view, namely

73

that the Ghost intervenes not to prevent Gertrude, but to prevent Hamlet, from doing something.

Dr. Bradley puts the question, "why does Shakespeare choose for the particular moment of its (the Ghost's) reappearance the middle of a speech in which Hamlet is raving against his uncle?"—and his answer is that Hamlet's father wishes to prevent his son from "agonizing his mother to no purpose". He goes on to say:

The object of his return is to repeat his charge:

> Do not forget: this visitation
> Is but to whet thy almost blunted purpose;

but, having uttered this reminder, he immediately bids the son to help the mother and "step between her and her fighting soul".

Prof. Stoll is of opinion that "the Ghost must appear again, and in the Queen's bed-chamber, not only because he did in the old play—otherwise a situation would be lost—but because the structure of the present one would be damaged. . . ." He quotes the Ghost's words: "do not forget . . . thy almost blunted purpose," and goes on to say:

> That light word is, in his judgment, enough . . . and the warrior-king, little impressed by his son's degeneracy, bids him comfort his mother.

No further explanation or interpretation of the Ghost's words is offered.

Mr. A. J. A. Waldock (in *Hamlet, A Study in Critical Method*, 1931) comes to the conclusion: "I see no clear way out of the trouble except (the last ludicrous and desperate measure left us) to refuse to take very much notice of the lines."

Professor Dover Wilson maintains that Hamlet is on

the point of disclosing to Gertrude the fact of his father's assassination; but, Dover Wilson goes on to say:

> . . . the fact of the murder must be kept from her, and the Ghost intervenes to prevent a revelation which would lay too heavy a burden of shame and guilt upon her.

But surely that revelation, supposing it to be one to her, can in no way lay that burden upon her: either she is innocent, then her conscience will remain untouched; or she is guilty, then shame and guilt lie already upon her soul.

Granville-Barker's view is this:

> Despite his father's bidding he is upon the point, in his rage, of telling his mother that her lover and husband was her husband's murderer, when the Ghost's reappearance prevents this.

Yet is Hamlet really on the point of disclosing anything at all? Looking through the text we find that he does not state any fact, nor prepares to do so; he merely abuses Claudius, calling him "villain . . . a cutpurse", etc. It must be because of Gertrude that the Ghost appears, on her behalf, or in view of something she is on the point of doing. He who has insight into souls, at least into Gertrude's soul, knows what is coming, and is determined to prevent it.

What he wishes to prevent—I suggest it once more— is her confession. For were it not so, there is no reason why he should appear at all. If Gertrude is innocent, is there any reason why she should not be told the truth? A widow is after all entitled—and has even the duty—to demand that she should be told how her husband met his death. Finding it out by herself, would she not heavily

75

reproach her son, and rightly so, for not telling her the truth? If on the other hand Gertrude is guilty, then there is no reason either why the "revelation" should be prevented since to her it is no revelation at all. Yet to Hamlet it would be a revelation indeed, were she to admit her guilt. It is this admission the Ghost has come to prevent.

And now, what is it the Ghost says? Hamlet addresses him asking whether he has come to chide him. To this his father answers briefly:

> Do not forget: this visitation
> Is but to whet thy almost blunted purpose.

One feels that this "whetting of purpose" is not the real reason for his appearance. Just now after the masterstroke of the Mouse-trap it is almost nonsense to speak of his son's "almost blunted purpose". Things are moving, vehemently so, moving to a dramatic climax—only moving, as the Ghost fears, in the wrong direction. He cannot be dissatisfied with Hamlet's "purpose" nor, just now, with its tempo or vigour; what he is worried about is its course. In fact, one has the impression that the second part of his speech is the real purpose of his intervention, and that, at the moment, his consideration for Gertrude is more vital to him than his desire for revenge. After those two lines he turns to the real object of his visit:

> But look, amazement on thy mother sits;
> O, step between her and her fighting soul,
> Conceit in weakest bodies strongest works.
> Speak to her, Hamlet.

He speaks of her "fighting soul". What is her soul fighting for?—or fighting against? Does not the word refer to her inner struggle whether or not she should admit her share in the murder?

*

76

THE GHOST'S HIC ET UBIQUE

Dr. Bradley has drawn attention to a scene in Thomas Heywood's *The Second Part of the Iron Age*, in which the Ghost of Agamemnon appears while Orestes and Clytemnestra are talking together: his son perceives him; to his wife he remains invisible. The parallel is very close and indeed more striking than Bradley himself would have been prepared to admit. The salient point is that Clytemnestra cannot see her husband's apparition because she has murdered him. The simplest explanation why old Hamlet remains invisible to Gertrude is the same: because she has murdered him.

Is there any better explanation for Gertrude's blindness?*

* Prof. Stoll's explanation is both simple and innocent; he maintains that the Ghost's "being visible to one person present and not another, that is as much a part of ghost-lore, Renaissance or ancient, as appearing at midnight, vanishing ere cock-crow. . . ."

VII

The Art of the "Perhaps"

"Did Claudius kill his brother?" Everybody, asked that question, would unhesitatingly answer: "Yes, of course." In this case Shakespeare himself clearly says: "yes." In the case of Gertrude, however, although he purposely causes us to ask the question, he neither says "yes" nor "no"; he says: "perhaps". There can be no doubt that his enigmatic silence is in no way due to any failure on the author's part to make things clear, but a deliberate and skilfully used feature of the scheme. (When Ibsen was asked whether in one of his plays a certain character did commit a certain crime, the old magician answered with a smile: "Possibly; I wouldn't put it past him.")

Let us first attempt to summarize all the evidence in the trial against Gertrude, and afterwards endeavour to find out why Shakespeare avoids committing himself to any clear answer. Advising a jury how to reach their verdict a judge might sum up the case as follows:

"The defendant is a clever, one might even say a shrewd, woman. She has been used to telling lies. She does not deny having committed adultery with the co-defendant Claudius. She does not lack personal courage. Thus it may be said that her character would not disallow her complicity in the murder.

In view of her morally weak disposition and the fact of her adultery it does not seem impossible that the defendant knew beforehand of the plan to murder the man to whom as his wife she was unfaithful. Nor is it impossible that she took an active part in the execution of it. More particularly it may have been that she withdrew from the orchard and left her husband unguarded in order to give the murderer free access to his victim.

78

These, however, are vague possibilities only. Somewhat more than possible—one might, perhaps, say probable—seems another reading of the facts: namely that she learned of the murder after it was done. It may be that on learning or, perhaps, on discovering the truth she was deeply and genuinely distressed. It may even be that she strove to dissociate herself from the crime and its perpetrator. Presently, however, she might have found out that on account of her illicit relations with the said Claudius she had no choice but to acquiesce in what had been done, although it may have been much against her better self. Her son, to whom otherwise she might have turned for intervention, was away at Wittenberg, and her lover, with his clandestinely gained power over her, may have threatened her with disclosure and thus blackmailed her into acceptance of the accomplished fact.

This interpretation seems to be consistent with her sullen behaviour and conspicuous reticence towards her second husband. Perhaps she was unable to see how she could free herself from the grip he apparently had on her. Even if she contemplated breaking with him there was no one to whom she could have turned for help. The murderer-husband was now king and held all power in his hands. She might have turned to her son; but he would have been powerless, his uncle having ascended the throne. Also she would have been compelled to confess to her own son the fact of her adultery, if not more. That might have been beyond her moral strength. And thus, finding no alternative, she had to go on bearing the burden of her guilt to the very end.

That, gentlemen of the jury, is the situation, factual and psychological, as we may assume it to have been. But to base your verdict on assumptions only would never do. If we ask what real evidence there is against the defendant we are compelled to say that there is nothing but her own confession, couched in somewhat obscure terms, that she is "afraid of being found out" and that "her guilt might betray itself". *Such a confession, in itself no evidence, cannot make up for the lack of any hard facts to which the confession could be related.*

Therefore, members of the jury, I should advise you . . ."

*

A verdict of "not proven", that is all a jury could arrive at. But even if, for lack of evidence, I am compelled to say "not guilty" as a juror, as a private individual I may still be convinced that the acquitted person has done the deed. So I feel in the case of Gertrude. As a juror I should have to acquit her; and yet it is my conviction that she knew of the murder all along and that she probably had consented to it.

In those "enlightened" adaptations of the play we find Gertrudes about whose guilt there is no question at all; they openly speak of it, confess and are punished. How weary, stale, flat, and uninteresting! Their authors differed from Shakespeare in their artistic as well as moral tenets: they did not like uncertainties or doubts; they were for either Yes or No, for black or white, for morality with reward or immorality with punishment. Something in between, something neither Yes nor No, or half Yes, half No—in one word: a "perhaps"— did not exist for them.

Shakespeare, at least the later Shakespeare, recognized the dramatic value of chiaroscuro and has learned to apply it. About the catastrophe that overtakes Lady Macbeth we hear only:

> The queen, my lord, is dead.

—and later Malcolm speaks of her:

> Who, as 'tis thought, by self and violent hands
> Took off her life . . .

—but we never learn any details of her death. The author prefers to leave them in the dark. He gives a stimulus to our imagination, but leaves it to ourselves to imagine how she might have met her end. Sometimes a question-mark seems to him better than any other punctuation.

In the case of Gertrude, Shakespeare did not want to be definite. It would, therefore, be a mistake for an actress to play a "guilty" Gertrude, no less so than to impersonate an "innocent" Gertrude. The part should be given in such a way that the audience suspect her right to the end, without ever solving the puzzle. Even after the performance, on their way home, they should ask themselves: "Did she do it—or did she not——?"

On some of Rembrandt's nocturnal pictures we find obscure figures lingering mysteriously in the dim background, figures whom we divine rather than see. They would scarcely stir our imagination were they properly drawn and clearly perceptible. And Goethe once said to his faithful Eckermann: "It is not the intellect to which a poetical work appeals: the more inscrutable it is, the better."

*

VIII

". . . BUT THIS IS WONDROUS STRANGE!"

AFTER the Closet-scene the Ghost does not appear any more. And since the Closet-scene has been dealt with, this book should by rights come to an end. Its title is *Hamlet's Father*, and as Hamlet's father has disappeared never to return, I too should leave the stage. Yet I am sure everybody would feel that to break off at this point would be absurd; it would leave the book a torso. Which only goes to show that the play does not cease to be the Ghost's play even after his final exit. He remains the moving power; whatever his son does, tries to do, is prevented from doing, and in the end fulfils, he acts throughout as his father's executor. It is, I should think, not enough to see Hamlet's difficulties alone; we should also, and first of all, see those of his father, which are greater. Hamlet fails; not before he himself is dying does he accomplish his duty. But stepping as it were on his son's dead body, the Ghost achieves his revenge.

The Closet-scene over, Hamlet seems to give up the race. He consents to be shipped to England; he returns, and instead of attacking the King he comes to blows with Laertes; instead of using his sword against Claudius he enters into a sword-play and is killed. All that is due to his failure to accomplish anything, which, according to so many critics, is the result of his inertia, forgetfulness, disobedience, shortsightedness. And yet:

> There's a divinity that shapes our ends,
> Rough-hew them how we will.

It is the divinity of right against evil that works in him and through him, even against his will. The torch may burn itself out; but the eternal light, the light of justice, can never be quenched. In this case it has been lit by the Ghost: he is the torch-bearer.

During the second part of the play, we have to admit, the light of the torch becomes more and more dim and almost reaches the point of extinction. Dr. Bradley speaks of Hamlet as fallen into

a kind of sad or indifferent self-abandonment, as if he secretly despaired of forcing himself to action, and were ready to leave his duty to some other power than his own.

And Dr. Johnson remarks:

After he has, by the stratagem of the play, convinced the King, he makes no attempt to punish him; and his death is at last effected by an incident which Hamlet has no part in producing.

This inactivity or lack of determination or whatever Hamlet's failure to act may be called has been commented upon by a host of critics, each in his own way. It would be impossible to give a complete list of their findings; but a few opinions, the most important on the one hand and the most recent on the other, may be useful to quote.

(1) *Goethe:* To me it is clear that Shakespeare sought to depict a great deed laid upon a soul unequal to the performance of it. . . . Here is an oak tree planted in a costly vase, which should have received into its bosom only lovely flowers: the roots spread out, the vase is shivered to pieces. . . . A beautiful, pure, noble, and most moral nature, without the strength of nerve which makes the hero, sinks beneath a burden which it can neither bear nor throw off; every duty is holy to him—this too hard. The impossible is required of him—not the impossible in itself, but the impossible to him.

83

(2) *Coleridge:* In Hamlet, Shakespeare seems to have wished . to exemplify the moral necessity of . . . an equilibrium between the real and the imaginary worlds. In Hamlet this balance is disturbed . . . Hamlet is brave and careless of death; but he vacillates from thought, and loses the power of action in the energy of resolve.

(3) *Hazlitt:* Hamlet . . . is not a character marked by strength of will or even passion, but by refinement of thought and sentiment. Hamlet is as little of the hero as a man can well be. . . . He seems incapable of deliberate action. . . .

(4) *E. K. Chambers:* The most tragic, the most affecting thing in the world is the ruin of a high soul. This is the theme of *Hamlet*; it is a tragedy of failure, of a great nature confronted with a low environment, and so, by the perversity of things, made ineffective and disastrous through its own greatness . . . he has lost the power of deliberate purposeful action. . . . He has turned the whole matter over and cannot decide. . . . The infinitely sad fate of Ophelia; the deaths of Polonius, Laertes, Gertrude, Rosencrantz, Guildenstern; for all their faults, all these are a sacrifice on the altar of his infirmity. . . . The ineffectiveness of the speculative intellect in a world of action, that is the key-note of the play. . . . The key-note of Hamlet's nature is the over-cultivation of the mind. . . . Claudius died justly, but—over and beyond Ophelia—the blood that is shed is at Hamlet's door.

Another group is headed by

(5) *Roderich Benedix:* The play is badly constructed . . . Shakespeare was not master of his material . . . Ophelia's madness is nothing but a stage effect. With such merely theatrical effects the play abounds, and that is why for so long it has succeeded in fascinating theatre-goers. Nevertheless, there is much that is good in the play. . . . All the clever attempts of so great a number of scholars to discover the heart of that mystery are

completely superfluous; for the obvious explanation of that mystifying puzzle lies in the simple fact that in the composition of the play Shakespeare has permitted himself a whole series of gross mistakes.

(6) *T. S. Eliot:* . . . so far from being Shakespeare's masterpiece, the play is most certainly an artistic failure . . . *Hamlet*, like the sonnets, is full of some stuff that the writer could not drag to light, contemplate, or manipulate into art. . . . We must simply admit that there Shakespeare tackled a problem which proved too much for him. Why he attempted it at all is an insoluble puzzle.

(7) *J. Dover Wilson:* In fine, we were never intended to reach the heart of the mystery. That it has a heart is an illusion; the mystery itself is an illusion; Hamlet is an illusion. . . . The character of Hamlet, like the appearance of his successive impersonators on the stage, is a matter of "make-up".

(8) *S. L. Bethell* (Shakespeare and The Popular Dramatic Tradition): There is a general lack of unity: the mad-scene, for example, focuses more attention on Ophelia than her comparative unimportance in the plot would warrant; it may have been included principally because mad-scenes were popular at the time. . . . *Hamlet* betrays frequent signs of immaturity and experiment. To dispute the strength and depth and brilliance of the play would be absurd; but as poetic drama it cannot compare with the later tragedies. Its greater popularity on the stage is due to sheer "entertainment value"; and it is a favourite with the critics because its imperfections leave more room for discussion, and the peculiar character of its hero provides a fascinating subject for every variety of arm-chair quackery.

(9) *Granville-Barker:* Here, for me, is the master-clue to Hamlet's "mystery". The "sane" world around him has naturally no sense in it, nor the too sane spectator of the play. He does not pluck out the heart of it himself.

Neither are we meant to. For his trouble is rooted in the fact that it is a mystery. (p. 327) . . . Shakespeare has not—paradox though this may seem—finally *dramatized* Hamlet. Here is the character, at which he had more than one immature and fragmentary try, fully and vividly imagined at last—what character was ever more so? But he does not submit it to the final discipline which would make it an integral part of the play. (p. 13) . . . Hamlet, the irresolute bungler . . . (p. 258) . . . such a weather-cock as Hamlet . . . (p. 276) Shakespeare has to reconcile the creature of his imagination with the figure of the borrowed story; the Hamlet we have is the tragic product of his very failure to do so. (p. 290.)*

These discordant voices enter in succession, as in a fugue, one higher, one lower; each carries the theme of "blunder" in his own way through variations and figurations; in the end they combine in a cacophonous chorus of "failure"—not Hamlet's, but Shakespeare's "failure". Horatio would say: "O day and night, but this is wondrous strange!"—and I feel as though I ought to apologize. Of course I knew that *Hamlet* has for long been the cause of great dissatisfaction amongst critics; and yet, before compiling the list just given, I had no idea that the sum total would be so enormous, especially among the modern authorities. I knew that as early a critic as Hanmer was at a loss to find any reason for Hamlet's procrastination; but then, he thought, had Hamlet "gone naturally to work there would have been an end to our play"—a conception that does away with the problem in the simplest possible manner. Dr. Johnson also was not too happy about the structure of the play; he was of opinion that "of the feigned madness of Hamlet there appears no adequate cause". Yet it was only with those two German critics, Goethe and Benedix—more dissimilar minds can

* Miss Edith Sitwell (in *A Notebook on William Shakespeare*) says that "*Hamlet* is a hunting story—that of a man who is hunting his own soul, or the truth of his own soul, and who never finds it."

hardly be imagined—that the business of fault-finding began in earnest.

Goethe—I am almost tempted to say "of course"—did not find any fault with the author of *Hamlet*. To him, to speak of "artistic failure" on Shakespeare's part would have seemed to be blasphemy. In his opinion Shakespeare intended to show how a noble nature breaks under too heavy a burden. Hamlet fails, but not his author.

In Goethe's footsteps followed, with occasional small deviations or additions, Schlegel, Coleridge, Hazlitt, and others. Sir E. K. Chambers turns fault into guilt: he accuses Hamlet of "sacrificing on the altar of his infirmity" so many lives; "the blood that is shed is at Hamlet's door."

The members of the second school are of opinion that not Hamlet, but Shakespeare failed. The founder of that school is Dr. Roderich Benedix, a dramatist, who in 1873 published a book called *The Shakespeare Mania*. In this book we find all the shoots that later sprouted so vigorously. If Mr. Eliot speaks of "artistic failure", there we have Benedix saying that the play is badly constructed. If the one "must admit" that in writing *Hamlet* Shakespeare "tackled a problem which proved too much for him", the other said long ago that Shakespeare was not master of his material. If Mr. Bethell thinks Ophelia's mad-scenes may have been included because mad-scenes were popular, we have old Benedix's word for it that Ophelia's madness is nothing but a stage effect. If the one does not dispute the strength and depth and brilliance of the play, the other does not deny either that there is much in *Hamlet* that is good. Both are convinced that the popularity of the play can only be ascribed to what the one calls "sheer entertainment value" and the other "merely theatrical effects".

And so it goes on; each subsequent voice tries to emulate if not to outbid those before him. If Benedix

87

asserts that it is completely superfluous to attempt to discover the heart of that mystery, Professor Dover Wilson maintains that the heart of the mystery is an illusion, the mystery itself is an illusion, Hamlet is an illusion. If Mr. Eliot speaks of Shakespeare's inability to manipulate his stuff into art in the same way as he "handled the suspicion of Othello, the infatuation of Antony", etc., we hear the echo from Mr. Bethell, who declares that as poetic drama *Hamlet* "cannot compare with the later tragedies". If Professor Dover Wilson says that "we were never intended to reach the heart of the mystery", Granville-Barker holds that Hamlet does not pluck out the heart of the mystery himself; "neither are we meant to." If Mr. Eliot thinks that in the case of *Hamlet* the writer was "unable to impose this motive" (the effect of a mother's guilt upon her son) "successfully upon the 'intractable' material of the old play", Granville-Barker takes up the theme by stating that Shakespeare had to reconcile the creature of his imagination with the figure of the borrowed story; "the Hamlet we have is the tragic product of his very failure to do so." Failure, failure again, nothing but failure!

(One thing in parentheses: The poets among the critics, reflecting on Hamlet, involuntarily achieve one thing: each of them shows his own face as if reflected in a mirror. It is highly significant of Goethe himself that he sees Hamlet as one to whom every duty is holy. It was Coleridge's main trouble that he was unable himself to find that "equilibrium between the real and the imaginary worlds". And it is characteristic of Mr. Eliot's own ways and methods that he speaks of Shakespeare as "dragging some stuff to light, contemplating, and manipulating it into art". It is as if the purpose of this play, to use Hamlet's own words, were to hold up a mirror to show virtue her own feature and scorn her own image.)

*

It seems indeed "wondrous strange" that such mordant criticism should have been levelled against a play that for three and a half centuries has been a success with the general public and that seems likely to remain so for another few years. Stranger still, that of these latest critics not one has been influenced by Goethe's perhaps old-fashioned yet reverent conception, but that one after the other they followed the path of disrespect and detraction which Dr. Benedix, that tedious realist, was the first to tread. To deliberate on this phenomenon and to ask whether the general tendency towards disparagement and denigration is not a symptom of our age (which, while seeking to smash idols, has spoiled and profaned so many sacred temples) would, interesting though it is, lie outside the scope of this inquiry.

Returning, then, to the subject, we find the following alternatives: If Shakespeare intends to show a young prince involved in difficulties and ending in failure, then it cannot be any failure on Shakespeare's part when he succeeds in showing that failure. On the other hand, if Shakespeare intends to show a prince who is a hero, strong and active, but who lets his creator down by shirking his duty and refusing to act, then it is Hamlet's failure and his alone. Yet the mere wording of that proposition demonstrates its absurdity: disobedience shown by Hamlet to his author is of course unthinkable. But what if the reason for Hamlet's inactivity is not disobedience to his creator, nor unwillingness to carry out his duty, nor any physical or psychological weakness? What if he is prevented from doing his duty because this duty, by its very nature, is impossible of execution? Then indeed would Hamlet be a hero, though one with his hands fettered, and the responsibility for his failure would lie not with him, nor with a blundering Shakespeare, but with the Ghost. That, in fact, is my contention.

*

Goethe remarks that Hamlet has no plan of his own, but that the play itself is nevertheless well planned. That Hamlet himself has no plan is true in the second half of the play only, where indeed the reins drop from his hands. But then Claudius takes them up and does all in his power to achieve his own downfall. (Thus it is always with the ministers of darkness.) The two schemes, Hamlet's action and Claudius's counteraction, are complementary; if we combine them the play seems indeed well planned.

(1) The Ghost reveals what has happened and imposes on his son the duty of revenge, qualifying the task by the injunction regarding Gertrude.

(2) Hamlet first wishes to find out whether the Ghost has spoken the truth, and achieves this by means of the Mouse-trap.

(3) On account of the dual nature of the task Hamlet cannot proceed straightaway; before acting against Claudius, he seeks to ascertain his mother's share in the crime. The Ghost, by his personal intervention, prevents him from doing so.

(4) Claudius, realizing that his crime has been discovered, is now roused to activity himself: he sends Hamlet to England, to immediate death. On learning that Hamlet has returned he arranges for his assassination in his mother's presence.

(5) Hamlet, finding his father's plan unworkable, fails to do anything. Claudius's counterplan succeeds, but he is caught in his own trap. Thus, by the very failure of the hero and the very success of the villain, final victory is won: victory for the principle of justice, represented in the Ghost.

It is the Ghost, and the wrong done to him, that starts the play; his desire to be avenged forms the content and the ethical purpose of the play; the avenger "lapses in time and passion": and yet, in spite of all, revenge is achieved, the wrong is righted.

*

IX

WEIGHED IN THE BALANCES

IF we wish to judge a coolie's strength, or endurance, or willingness we must first find out the weight of the load he carries, or breaks under, or refuses to lift. In a similar way, before we can either praise or censure Hamlet's endeavours we ought to scrutinize the burden laid upon him by his father.

At first sight the two parts of the task seem to be easy enough: (*a*) "revenge" and (*b*) "nothing against Gertrude". Yet if one tries to put oneself in Hamlet's place the aspects change: not only is each of the two parts more than difficult in itself; combined, they prove to be simply impossible; in fact, they cancel each other.

The first command seems simplicity itself: "Son, I have been murdered: revenge my death!" And then? Could Hamlet have gone and run a rapier through the murderer? Physically, no doubt, he could have done so; and in fact some of his critics admit their failure to understand why he did not go to work without more ado and have done with it. But what, had he so acted, would have been the result? First, no later than at the beginning of the second act, to use Hanmer's words, "there would have been an end to our play". Yet putting aside that somewhat too easy interpretation: what would have been Hamlet's position? Having slain his uncle, he would have proclaimed that his deed was revenge, the legitimate punishment of his father's murder. But who would have believed him?

The victim of his action would have been the reigning king, for months in undisputed possession of the throne, married to the late king's widow. It would have been a case of plain, unqualified regicide. Obviously Rosencrantz, Guildenstern and all others present would

91

have set upon him and killed him on the spot. (Just as
the "Danes" in that Vienna adaptation of the play
would have done, only that there the Queen intervened
and, with the full confession of her own guilt, acted as
chief witness for her son.) Yet even had they merely
arrested Hamlet and tried him for high treason and
murder, whom could he have called in as witness—except
(perhaps) his mother?

He would have referred to the Ghost and told his judges
that the apparition, in a private talk after midnight, had
revealed to him the fact of the murder. He might just as
well have told them that his father had appeared to him
in a dream; it would have made the same impression on his
judges: they would probably have laughed. In order to
convince them, could he have produced his witness in
court? And even if, at his son's bidding, the Ghost had
actually appeared before them and repeated his story,
would the judges have believed him? Would they not
have been in doubt, just as Hamlet himself had been,
whether the Ghost was a good or an evil spirit, whether his
accusation was true or not? How could the Ghost have
convinced them of his own credibility?

No other way would have been open to confirm the
truth but by obtaining the murderer's confession.
Claudius's own words or, since that was not to be hoped
for, his self-betrayal would have been the only means of
saving the defendant. But a dead Claudius, rashly slain,
could have neither confessed his deed nor betrayed himself:
and thus for Hamlet, the regicide, there would have been
nothing but the gallows. (The considerations just offered
suggest that the Mouse-trap, with the King's self-betrayal
as its object, was probably the only way in which Hamlet
could hope to discover whether the Ghost had spoken
the truth or not.)

But—some of the critics seem to think—why should
Hamlet have hesitated to kill Claudius, even at the risk

of being hanged and quartered for it? By doing so he would at least have acted and, moreover, acted as a loyal and obedient son. There is little doubt that Laertes, had he been in Hamlet's position, would have acted in this way, following the principle: first do the deed, and let the reasons for it look after themselves. Yet it is obvious that Shakespeare depicts Laertes as an impulsive hothead in order to contrast him with Hamlet. In the one case he wishes to show an unscrupulous weakling—for such is Laertes—who obeys the urge of the moment and is easily swayed even into committing a cowardly crime; in the other he gives us a genuine prince who, with his innate nobility and conscientiousness, had he ascended the throne would have "proved most royally".

Being the man he is, Hamlet sees it as his duty to take vengeance; but he does not wish to debase himself by becoming an assassin. That is what is in his mind when (in III. 3), finding the King on his knees, he refuses to kill him. He explains it clearly enough; he says:

O, this is hire and salary, not revenge.

He desires to act as judge; not as a hired murderer or a salaried executioner.*

There is yet another point. Hamlet is scrupulous not merely for the sake of being scrupulous, but for the sake of his reputation. Almost with his last breath he implores Horatio to absent himself from felicity awhile so that he may tell his story:

O good Horatio, what a wounded name,
Things standing thus unknown, shall live behind me!

And once more, already at his last gasp, he asks Horatio to tell Fortinbras——:

* See Appendix, Note E.

93

So tell him, with th' occurrents, more and less,
Which have solicited . . . the rest is silence.

It is evident that Hamlet has a passionate desire to be
justified, not merely before himself, but before the world.
Seeing that he cares so eagerly for his good name even
after death, can we imagine that he would grasp a dagger
and madly thrust it into his enemy? The situation, his
judicial mind, his whole nature, all hold him back from
slaying Claudius out of hand.

There are other considerations as well. The man is
defenceless: morality speaks against choosing such a
moment. He is, so Hamlet must assume, deep in prayer:
religion speaks against it. And there is, foremost among
the other reasons, his desire (more burning than his desire
for revenge) to make sure of his mother's share in the crime.
Called upon, as he feels he is, to act as judge, it would have
been impossible for him to proceed to any final judgment
before knowing the respective parts the two had played
in the performance of the murder. He is just on his way
to his mother's room; in a few minutes, he thinks, he will
know all. He cannot now stop and overthrow his whole
plan, which is, to pursue a course of judicial inquiry. Nor
can he depart from the ethical ground of his duty by
acting as brutal chance suggests to him: by committing
murder. He is not another Laertes.

Finally, there is his father's injunction not to contrive
anything against his mother; of this, more will have to be
said presently.

*

But why—the objection is sure to be raised—why does
Hamlet omit to state his reasons plainly and frankly?
His critics are all agreed that in his soliloquy: "Now might
I do it pat . . ." he gives pretexts instead of his true

94

An 18th century arrangement of the Mouse Trap scene
(The costumes are contemporary.)

"The Mouse Trap," as arranged in Berlin, 1778

(The simplest solution: no one as much as glances at the Dumb-show, not even the "Switzers".)

"The Mouse Trap"

(From the Two Cities film, produced at Denham, with Sir Laurence Olivier as Hamlet.)

Joseph Lange as Hamlet in Vienna, 1773
(Lange's brother-in-law was Mozart.)

Sir Henry Irving as Hamlet
(From a Marble statue by E. Onslow Ford in the Guildhall, London.)

Sir Laurence Olivier in the closet scene, seeing his
father's ghost
(From the Two Cities film production of *Hamlet* at Denham.)

Sir Laurence Olivier during the fencing match
(From the Two Cities film production of *Hamlet* at Denham.)

motives. In a sense that is so. At times we have the impression that he offers us the trimmings only of his thoughts, not the dish itself. Does he not wish to say what he thinks or is he unable to do so? Does he try to deceive us or does he deceive himself?

Iago, who has one thing in common with Hamlet, namely his shrewd intellect, goes to work differently. He explains his motives and intentions quite openly. He always has a plan which he rolls out in front of himself as if it were a piece of carpet to walk on; we can see what it is and how far it stretches. Iago always tries to clarify things, to himself as well as to us. Round Hamlet, however, round his motives and intentions, there is almost always an aura of twilight. On so many occasions we grope in half-darkness because Hamlet himself—at least we think so—is groping in the dark. And yet, there is on the other hand his penetrating shrewdness, the sharpness of his wit, his irony, his sensitiveness, his almost uncanny insight into the psychology of others: how, we ask ourselves, is all that compatible with the cloudy gloom that so often appears to darken his path?

Hamlet, it seems to me, is always one jump ahead of himself. His mind does not walk, but moves by leaps and bounds. That in itself is nothing extraordinary; the unusual thing, however, is that he is continually one jump further than he ought to be. When we expect him to deliberate whether or not to commit suicide he does not think of dying, but of being dead. Death is no problem to him: but what may happen after death, that worries him. When he is actually on the point of dying he is concerned with the problem of the succession: Fortinbras has his "dying voice". The sight of skulls would cause everybody to muse on mortality; Hamlet must go further and ruminate on how bones will fall to dust and dust transform into loam and loam stop a beer-barrel. Polonius's body, dead for a few hours only, is not yet buried; but

95

Hamlet sees it already eaten by worms. Claudius speaks of his own good purposes. "Purposes"—that is what really counts on doomsday—and at once Hamlet replies: "I see a Cherub that sees them."

In this way his mind works throughout. It seems as though he were longsighted: he does not see what is nearest to him, but is interested in the distance only. The nearest reason, the nearest motive is not worth caring or speaking about, but is swept aside. What lies beyond it is all that matters, is all that must be seized. Goethe said once: "Because they are talking to me in Weimar they think I am with them; but I am already in Jena."

This being so, should we not expect Shakespeare to give us a warning of this peculiarity in his hero's mind? Actually there is such a warning, and we find it exactly where we should look for it: in the first real speech Hamlet makes: the proper place for the first preliminary self-revelation. When Gertrude uses the word "seems" Hamlet (I. 2. 76) snaps back:

"Seems", madam? Nay, it is: I know not "seems" . . .

The line is truly characteristic of that somewhat self-assured, slightly arrogant and presumptuous young mind. (For Hamlet is young, very young, whatever his years.) For him, outward appearances do not exist; what is behind the outward form, that only counts. He prides himself on his mind that penetrates to the interior of things, nay, even works its way through appearances to what lies hidden behind them.

This self-confidence, built upon his intellectual self-reliance, is the basis of his solitary and yet completely sagacious conduct of the duty laid upon him. He does not blindly trust the message from beyond: so he first ascertains the true character of the Ghost. That done, he does not

96

feel satisfied with what the Ghost has chosen to tell him: so he makes for his mother's room to find out the rest of the story. He is determined on that; he had said to himself:

Soft now, to my mother:

—and when on his way that chance is offered him, the chance of assassinating the assassin, he is for a moment tempted by it; but almost instantly his mind veers back and, as usual, jumps ahead. What if he should do it? Would not his victim's soul fly up to heaven?—and so forth. What he actually says is neither pretext nor deceit; it is a genuine part of his thought: only that the chief part is omitted. The most immediate reasons, as is his habit, he has jumped; about these he does not talk.

Now, had all gone according to plan, Hamlet would have extorted from his mother the confession of her guilt and then, with everything cleared up, would have proceeded against his uncle. Yet events take a different course. His father intervenes; Gertrude's confession is prevented; and Claudius, exploiting Polonius's death, sends Hamlet away. Thus the first part of the Ghost's command comes to an end: the command of revenge ends in frustration.

*

The second part is: "nothing against Gertrude". Is that part easier to fulfil?

Had Hamlet without delay done Claudius to death, the enraged courtiers would have killed him instantly: thus he would have robbed his mother both of her husband and of her only son. Would that have meant doing nothing against his mother? But let us assume that he survived the assassination: tried for murder he would have been compelled to tell his judges of the Ghost's accusation against Gertrude, which would have meant dragging her down into the mire of public dishonour. The same would have been the case had he proceeded against Claudius in the judicial manner he had actually chosen. Whichever turn he took he would have had to disclose his mother's adultery, if not more than this.

To contrive everything against the murderer but nothing against the adulteress was impossible. To do nothing against the adulteress would have meant dropping all proceedings against the murderer. The problem was truly insoluble. The task itself was of such a nature that no one in the world would have been able to carry it out. To act against one person who is one half of a couple, but not to act against the other person who is the other part of the couple, is an impossibility in itself.

*

Yet even assuming that, despite everything, it had been possible for Hamlet to do what his father had asked of him, it is now too late. He is arrested.

Of the fact that he is actually put under arrest there can be no doubt. Claudius sends Rosencrantz and Guildenstern after him, and says expressly (IV. I. 33):

. . . join you with some further aid.

—meaning apparently the assistance of his "Switzers". When (in IV. 2) the two friends meet Hamlet, who has just "safely stowed" Polonius's body, they are very curt, relying more on the strength of the halberds behind them than on the strength of their friendship.

What have you done, my lord, with the dead body?
. . .
Tell us where 'tis . . .
. . .

98

My lord, you must tell us where the body is, and go
with us to the King.

The affability of the smiling school-fellows has vanished.
They have lowered themselves so deeply as to become
jailors. If the stage-producer fully exploits their despicable
behaviour (by making them speak in an insolent manner,
by letting the Switzers come threateningly near, etc.) the
audience will more easily understand why Hamlet is so
little concerned about their certain death in England. In
this scene we must arrive at the conviction, which Hamlet
evidently has formed, that the two good friends, now
completely subservient to Claudius, do not care two
straws about Hamlet's life.

In the following scene we see more clearly still that
Hamlet is a prisoner. When Claudius asks where he is,
Rosencrantz replies:

Without, my lord, guarded to know your pleasure.

Not only "guarded", but "guarded to know your pleasure",
which obviously means "to hear your judgement". Claudius
does not say: "bid him enter" or something similarly
polite; he gives the order:

Bring him before us.

—and Rosencrantz repeats it:

Ho, Guildenstern! Bring in my lord.

This "bringing in" should be a severe business. Hamlet
is certainly neither bound nor manacled. True, he is a
"madman" and has in a fit of homicidal mania slain old
Polonius; yet he is still a prince, and he is Queen
Gertrude's son. All the same, I think he should be

99

escorted in such a way, either with his arms seized by
two Switzers or else so closely guarded, that he is
prevented from attacking the King—who, moreover,
keeps carefully out of Hamlet's reach. He has just said:

How dangerous is it that this man goes loose!

There is yet another change in Claudius's attitude. So
far he has always, when addressing his nephew, used the
word "you"; now, throughout this scene, he says "thou"
to him. Whether this "thou" is meant to indicate contempt of, or condescension to, the madman; or whether it
is an involuntary sign of suppressed wrath I would not
venture to decide. It all depends upon whether the actor
shows his enmity to Hamlet openly or still conceals it
behind the smiling villain's indefatigable suavity. It is
in any case an indication of a decisive psychological
change in Claudius.

*

Here, then—and apparently until he boards the ship
for England—Hamlet is a prisoner. Even his strongest
intention to attack the King would have been too late.
He could have accused him in words, could have cried
out: "thou damned incestuous beast, thou murderer";
but nobody would have believed him, as he had proved
himself to be a homicide and mentally deranged.

Thus the two gaze at each other, with hatred blazing
in their eyes. Claudius knows that his crime has been
discovered, that Hamlet knows it, and that his madness
is merely a stratagem. Hamlet knows that Claudius
knows that he is discovered; but he knows also that he
cannot "contrive aught" against his uncle, just as he
cannot do anything against his mother. The whole plan
as laid upon him by his dead father is unworkable; it has

come to nothing. And now, to make things still worse, he is a prisoner and sent overseas.

A failure, most certainly a failure But is it Hamlet's failure? Why does he fail? Is there any lack of physical courage in him? Or lack of moral determination? Is he infirm of purpose? Up to the Mouse-trap he has acted in complete wisdom, adapting himself to the situation with courage and determination. That he forgoes to assassinate the praying King is the only thing to do, at least for him, who desires to act as judge and not as a "hired and salaried" murderer. That he wishes to extort from his mother the confession of her guilt is due to the fact that the Ghost has told him only half the story. There is nothing of which Hamlet can justly be accused. That he fails to carry out the revenge is entirely due to the impossibility of the task as such.

And so, nothing achieved, Hamlet sails for England.

*

X

An Interruption

Does Hamlet really sail? After his most effective farewell ("Farewell, dear mother . . . Come, for England!") we should expect to lose sight of him for some time. But no; he has hardly left before he appears again, to have first a talk with a Captain and then a soliloquy.

It is evident that after IV. 3 the stage needs a "broom", by which I mean that, before the next main scene can be played, the stage must be cleared or neutralized. Scene IV. 2, in which Hamlet is arrested by his school-fellows, was obviously given on the upper stage. During the first ten lines of the following scene (IV. 3), in which Claudius explains the situation to his "wisest friends", Hamlet, guarded, is brought downstairs and enters below to be banished from the country. The next scene to be played on the same lower stage is IV. 5, with first Gertrude and Horatio, later the distracted Ophelia, then Claudius, and finally the rebellious Laertes—a scene impossible to be given on the balcony. So between IV. 3 and IV. 5 there must be either a short scene on the upper stage, with the effect of the lower stage being neutralized, or there must be, on the lower stage itself, a "broom" to sweep away the locality of IV. 3, so that Gertrude and Horatio, on entering, can bring with them their own locality. Did IV. 5 follow immediately on IV. 3, the audience would have the impression of continuity, and continuity not of locality only but of time also. Either would be contrary to Shakespeare's intentions.

Of course you cannot show an "army" marching over the balcony, however small the "army". But there is no reason why a dozen soldiers should not have marched across the lower stage. An army is always in the open, and no one in the audience would suspect those "two thousand souls" of marching through Claudius's palace. For the few minutes during which they are present the stage is a country road. When, the scene over, Gertrude and Horatio enter we are at once back again in the palace. The cæsura brought about by the army's appearance has the added advantage of marking an indefinite lapse of time.

For this "broom"-scene Shakespeare introduces Fortinbras. It is high time for him to do so. So far Fortinbras has only been spoken of. But he will be needed for the ending of the play, and it would be awkward to bring in a completely new character just for the last few minutes. So Fortinbras enters, and since there is no one to introduce him he has to do that himself, telling us his name:

> Go, Captain, from me greet the Danish King,
> Tell him that by his licence *Fortinbras*
> Craves the conveyance of a promis'd march. . . .

With those two aims achieved, "sweeping" of the stage and introducing a new character, we should expect the scene to come to its end. And so it does—in the Folio. There we have:

> *Cap.* I will do't, my lord.
> *For.* Go softly on.

They exeunt.

In Quarto 2, however, strange things occur. We should assume that the Captain, a single person, charged with a message to the Danish King, would leave first. But it is Fortinbras who with all his "army" goes off and leaves the Captain behind. Then "Enter Hamlet, Rosencrantz, etc.". They miss Fortinbras, but meet the Captain. Strange; yet stranger still that Hamlet, having missed him, speaks of Fortinbras as if he had seen him: he calls him, a minute or two later, "a delicate and tender prince".

After he had talked to Hamlet, the Captain goes off and Rosencrantz invites the prince:

Wil't please you goe my Lord?

But Hamlet declines; he wants to soliloquize; and since it is customary to be alone when making a soliloquy he sends Rosencrantz away; he simply asks him:

Ile be with you straight, goe a little before.

Strange that Rosencrantz leaves him. Is he not in charge of a prisoner? And, after all, where are they? On the road. But should they not be on board ship, or embarking? That's right, the commentators say; they are "on their way to the harbour". Yet the text has nothing that would as much as hint at embarkation. In fact, the conversation with the Captain (which has the only purpose to lead up to the soliloquy) lies entirely outside the frame of the action; the soliloquy itself hangs in the air.

Yet strange as these things are, still stranger is the contents of the soliloquy. In itself it is a very fine speech indeed; if we try, however, to fit it into the texture of the play it appears to be completely foreign.

Hamlet had just had to acknowledge utter defeat. He is unable to achieve anything. He has succeeded in ascertaining that the Ghost's story was true; but everything else has gone amiss. Not only has the nature of the task made revenge impossible; he has now been arrested, led away under guard and is—so the critics say—on his way to be shipped overseas. In this situation, indisputably clear in its sad frustration and complete hopelessness, Hamlet is presented as stopping and making a speech in which he pronounces the following sentiments and intentions:

How all occasions . . . spur my dull revenge. . . .

Just now and here, on his way to England, how can he
speak any longer of the "dullness" of his revenge? He
asks himself what the reason may be for his procrastination:

> . . . whether it be
> Beastial oblivion, or some craven scruple. . . .

He does not say: "whether it *was*"; he says: "whether it
be," as though the chance of revenge were still open to him.

> . . . I do not know
> Why yet I live to say "This thing's to do" . . .

But all is over! Where does he intend to do "this thing"?
In England?

> Sith I have cause, and will, and strength, and means
> To do't . . .

"Strength and means to do't"? On his way into exile?

> . . . Examples, gross as earth, exhort me. . . .

But all exhortations are now too late.

> . . . How stand I, then,
> That have a father kill'd, a mother stain'd,
> Excitements of my reason and my blood,
> And let all sleep?

But the time for awakening what he had allowed to
"sleep" is irrevocably past!

> . . . O, from this time forth,
> My thoughts be bloody, or be nothing worth!

Where does he intend to let his "thoughts be bloody"?
In England? What help will they be to him there?

Again, as long as we look at this soliloquy as a piece of
rhetoric it is fine and persuasive; as soon, however, as we
try to connect it with what went before and what is to
follow, i.e., as soon as we examine it as dramatic speech it
appears to be completely out of place.

And that is what I submit it to be: the soliloquy is in
fact out of place.

I do not suggest that it is an interpolation by some
other hand; there seems to be no reason why it should
not be ascribed to Shakespeare himself. But I do think
that originally he meant to use it in some other connection: in a scene either before the idea of the Mouse-trap
was conceived or after Hamlet's return from his sea-
voyage; and that the author dropped it when, in the
course of writing or rewriting, he changed his plans.
However that may be, in no case can the soliloquy (and
the preceding dialogue) have been written for the place
where the editor of the Quarto text has put it. Each of
the passages quoted above speaks against that location.
The strongest evidence in favour of my suggestion, however, is the fact that the Folio text omits both dialogue
and monologue altogether. And Heminge and Condell,
Shakespeare's fellow-actors, can be trusted to have known
what they were doing.

For which context that supererogatory text was written;
why it was rejected in the end; how it came to be included
in the Quarto; whether the editor of the Quarto text
found that single page among the "foul papers" of the
manuscript and did not know where to put it: to speculate
on these questions would be idle and, in any case, go
beyond the limits of the present inquiry.

However, dialogue and soliloquy are to be found in
every edition of the play since Rowe and Pope. That they
have been included in the "accepted" text is easily

understood. The editors apparently thought it a pity to omit a monologue that has the true ring both of Shakespeare and Hamlet. And indeed it would be a pity to forgo so beautiful and, as to Hamlet's character, so revealing a passage. But why not put it into the Appendix, which is the right place for such paralipomena? I myself have done so. For my translation of *Hamlet*—published in Vienna in 1937—I decided to give the Folio and no other text. Accordingly the main text of my version does not contain those passages; nor for that matter the other small passages, in the Closet-scene and elsewhere, that the Folio has omitted. All of them, however, appear in an Appendix, introduced by the necessary explanations. Something similar might be done in English editions.

In any case, the dialogue and soliloquy in question, although they cannot be called extraneous, have certainly not been woven into the dramatic texture of the play. They are a patch sewn on by someone who found it and did not know that it was not meant to be used; at least not where he put it. We should, I think, adhere to the Folio, which—here as almost everywhere else—contains the final text.*

After this interruption let us return to the main subject.

*

* *See* Appendix, *Note F.*

XI

ONE JUMP AHEAD—ONE STEP TOO FAR

HAMLET sails for England—and with his departure the play seems to break up. As all of us know, *Hamlet* without the Prince of Denmark is not the right thing. True, while he is away we are shown what those critics mean who speak of "entertainment value" or "variety show", namely Ophelia's madness and Laertes's turbulent return. Either event is the direct outcome of Hamlet's rashness in slaying Polonius, and thus it is that the prince, though out of sight, is hardly ever out of the play. Still, for some time the scales of the play hold a somewhat unsteady balance: Hamlet's action has come to nothing and the King's counteraction has not yet begun. For Claudius there is no need to do anything except to assuage Laertes's wrath. That done, he would wait until the news reaches him from England of Hamlet's execution—and there indeed would be "an end to our play". Instead of this he receives Hamlet's letter, and his counterplan is set afoot at once.

Now, if ever there was a point in *Hamlet* for which its author might be censured it is the means by which those two parts, action and counteraction, are hinged together. At first sight it seems as though the provision of that hinge had been left to mere chance. Chance, however, should not be made an active force in tragedy, first of all for the practical reason that people are too easily induced to ask: "What course would things have taken without that accident?" And that question, or even the silent thought, is awkward because it distracts the audience's attention from the action itself and causes their minds to stray.

In fact, without the incident with the pirates Hamlet would have reached England as did the others; Rosen-

crantz and Guildenstern would have been beheaded—and
then? Would Hamlet have stayed in England and raised
a force strong enough to invade Denmark? Or would he
have sent messages to Fortinbras with the suggestion to
overthrow Claudius? Would he have been able to convince
the English, or Fortinbras, of the truth of the Ghost's
story and the righteousness of his own cause? But it is
idle to speculate on these questions (which only show
once more the difficulties that surround Hamlet wherever
he goes) since questions and difficulties have been avoided
by just that incident. Now, were this incident really one
of mere chance we should have to say, with however much
regret, that Shakespeare in this case made use of a somewhat shady expedient. But is it really one of blind
chance? A "mere accident", as Bradley calls it? Professor
Allardyce Nicoll (in *Studies in Shakespeare*) says that
Hamlet "eventually executes his purpose almost by
chance".

This book being mainly concerned with the Ghost, I
have as far as possible omitted dealing with Hamlet's
personality as such, i.e., separated from the general
layout of my inquiry. In Chapter IX, however, I have
spoken of Hamlet as being always one jump ahead of
everyone else. When I used that phrase there, I had no
intention of preparing the ground for what I am going to
say here. But now as the "pirate of very warlike appoint-
ment" sails up from the horizon, chasing Hamlet's ship,
I am myself surprised to find how a mental peculiarity
translates itself into motion. Hamlet's mental characteristic of always being "one jump ahead" leads him to a
real jump ahead of the others. As his letter describes it:

Finding ourselves too slow of sail, we put on a compelled valour. In the grapple, I boarded them: On the
instant they got clear of our ship, so I alone became their
prisoner.

What followed is obvious enough. The pirates, realizing what a valuable prize had fallen into their hands, sent two of their company with letters, apparently demanding ransom, and it is fairly clear that Claudius had to put a good face on a bad business and pay a handsome sum for the release of his nephew.

Everything would have been different and Claudius might have safely got away with crime, crown, and Queen, had not the pirates made that unexpected prisoner. Yet they would never have captured him, had it not been for his particular mentality, which caused him to jump over to their ship unnecessarily and ahead of all the others. In these circumstances to speak of blind chance does not seem to be justified.

Still, nothing would happen even after his return and the play would come to a standstill were it left to Hamlet to carry the action any further. For him the situation is still the same and his task, accordingly, still impossible of execution. He cannot avenge his father's death without exposing his mother to utter humiliation. The only thing he can do is to wait for any change in the situation, likely to offer him a chance to act—and that is what he does.

He has not long to wait. Even before his return to the palace Claudius has laid his plans. In his case, too, it seems mistaken to speak of blind chance. Just as it is Hamlet's "jumping ahead" that leads him back, so it is the King's mind that effects the turn of events. He suggests that in the sword-play Laertes should use "a sword unbated". Laertes consents at once and announces that in addition he would "anoint" his sword with poison. This double plot should be sufficient: the two fencers would kill each other, but he, Claudius, would escape. For although he does not realize it, as long as Gertrude is alive he, being her husband, is in no danger; but the moment she is dead, Hamlet's hands are free—and he uses them at once.

In his anxiety, however, to get rid of the witness and avenger, and not being held back by any qualms of conscience, Claudius is not content with what Laertes has undertaken to do: he goes one step further—and with that one step he brings about his own undoing. As a third means of killing Hamlet he decides to use poisoned wine. Gertrude drinks of it; she dies—and with her death Hamlet, although dying himself, regains his freedom of action: he kills Claudius—and thus it is that the murderer dies a victim of his own treachery. His plan, as Horatio puts it, falls on the inventor's head.

This one step too far and that one jump ahead, which between them bring about the final catastrophe, are not fortuitous but psychological. They are part of the emotional network of the play.

*

III

XII

THE DOOR INTO THE OPEN

IT was unavoidable to draw a parallel between Hamlet's jumping into the pirate ship and Claudius's overloading the murder plot; thus I had to anticipate the end. But here we have to go back again to the situation in which Hamlet finds himself when, returned from his adventures at sea and in the graveyard, he once more enters his father's palace.

When Hamlet had left for England he and Claudius were deadly foes. Either had reason to conceal before the Court what they really felt for one another. Claudius had no wish to make his own crime known, and Hamlet had to be silent for his mother's sake. But between themselves there was no doubt as to the nature of their feelings and intentions.

The voyage to England has miraculously ended in Hamlet's return. How does this fact influence the further relations between the two enemies? Claudius had not been content with banishing his nephew from Denmark; he had ordered his execution, despite the fact that far away in England Hamlet would have hardly been in a position to do anything against his uncle, the Danish King, England's overlord. If he so feared his nephew notwithstanding the sea between the two countries, how much more afraid of him must he be now when his foe is back again in Denmark, back at the Court!

On the other hand, for Hamlet too the situation has worsened. When he was shipped to England he might have taken it that the King merely wanted to have him out of the way. Now, however, having read the order for his execution, he must be aware that, at the first opportunity open to him, his uncle will seek to destroy him.

Added to this enmity, deadly, inescapable, implacable,

112

Hamlet has just brought on himself another. He had, although by accident, slain Polonius. He must have known, and certainly did know, that for this deed Laertes would call him to account. Instead of doing everything in his power to conciliate Laertes he gives way to a nervous outburst and comes to blows with him—over the coffin in which Ophelia lies, she for whose madness and death her brother rightly holds him responsible. True, Hamlet had at once thought better of it and tried to pacify him:

> Hear you, sir:
> What is the reason that you use me thus?
> I loved you ever. . . .

—but Laertes, it seems, had only turned from him; whereupon Hamlet had abused him grossly:

> . . . but it is no matter:
> Let Hercules himself do what he may,
> The cat will mew and dog will have his day.

Such is Hamlet's return. Two enemies are waiting for him: the one, the country's ruler, bent on seeking his life; the other demanding vengeance for father and sister. No time has passed since that grotesquely sinister scene in the graveyard. Scarcely has he finished telling Horatio his story when Osric appears. Osric had not yet had any occasion to see the Prince; in fact his first words are:

> Your lordship is right welcome back to Denmark.

And this Osric, within so short a time after the grave-yard incident, delivers an invitation . . . from whom? from the King; an invitation to a fencing-match . . . with whom? with Laertes.

Now, the question is: are we to believe that, while hearing, grasping and accepting that invitation, Hamlet has suddenly been seized by a fit of idiocy? Is he momentarily paralysed by a complete black-out of his mental faculties? Can we really assume that he does not see, smell, perceive that his enemies must have designs upon him? In a word, are we to take it that Hamlet walks blindly into the trap they have laid for him?

It is not without consequence how we answer that question. It makes all the difference whether Hamlet is slain treacherously, or whether he fights for his life, fully aware what he is doing, and doing it with the courage of a real hero. Does Hamlet permit his enemies to trip him up? to push him into his grave by a mean trick? Would it not be more in his line to make a last stand, though he knows he is doomed, and refuse to sell his life cheaply? In the so-called fencing-match, is he blind to the danger or is he looking Death straight in the face? Is he playing or is he fighting?

*

Bradley declares that "there is something noble in his (Hamlet's) carelessness", and he speaks of "that trustfulness which makes us love him".

Professor Dover Wilson is of opinion that our hero shows nobility and weakness in the business of the fencing-match, "which Hamlet ought never to have undertaken and by means of which the catastrophe is effected." And he goes on:

We love him for the very carelessness with which he falls in with the designs of his enemies, culpable as that carelessness is. . . .

Granville-Barker thinks that Hamlet "falls only in with it" (his enemies' plan) "in impatient indifference".

But surely neither of these interpretations can be reconciled with what we know of Hamlet's mind and character. He is rash in slaying Polonius, rash in boarding the pirate ship, rash in jumping into Ophelia's grave and at Laertes's throat. Yet when he learns of the appearance of a ghost he is incredulous and almost cross-examines the three witnesses. When he hears the Ghost's story he doubts both the teller's origin and his veracity. When Rosencrantz and Guildenstern approach him seemingly as casual visitors he suspects them almost at once. In fact, his want of trust is so remarkable—even before he is convinced of his uncle's crime—that suspiciousness may be said to be one of the main features of his mind.*

This mental peculiarity of his must become more marked still after the two events that expose to him the King's character in its whole frightfulness: his self-betrayal in the Mouse-trap and his letter to England. Of course Hamlet now knows that for him to trust Claudius even in the smallest matter would be like putting his head between a crocodile's jaws and hoping for the best. And yet, when that invitation is delivered, the invitation to fight—with "rapier and dagger"—with none other than Laertes, we are invited to accept the view that Hamlet falls in with his enemies' designs out of "culpable carelessness" or "impatient indifference".

If we exclude carelessness and indifference, as I think we must, what is Hamlet's attitude to that invitation? If he has retained his mental faculties, then he cannot but suspect foul play. My suggestion is that with open-eyed awareness he knows that in all likelihood he is going to his death.

*

Let us, first of all, have recourse to Hamlet's own words.

* Prof. J. Q. Adams thinks that Hamlet "would *never* suspect ill in others". Hamlet, he says, "does not for a moment question the friendly character of this match with Laertes . . . he falls a victim to his own nobility of character rather than to melancholia."

What does he say about the "fencing-match" and its probable outcome? He comforts Horatio, who, it is obvious, does not see as clearly as his princely friend:

> I shall win at the odds. But thou would'st not think how all here about my heart—but it is no matter.
>
> *Hor.:* Nay, my good lord——
>
> *Ham.:* It is but foolery! But it is such a kind of gain-giving as would perhaps trouble a woman.
>
> *Hor.:* If your mind dislike anything, obey. I will forestall their repair hither, and say you are not fit.
>
> *Ham.:* Not a whit—we defy augury! There's a special providence in the fall of a sparrow. If it be now, 'tis not to come: if it be not to come, it will be now: if it be not now, yet it will come. The readiness is all. Since no man has ought of what he leaves—what is't to leave betimes?
>
> *Enter King, Queen, Laertes . . .*

(The text is that of the Folio, only modernized in spelling and punctuation.)

Hamlet speaks of his own death. How else can we explain his "gain-giving as would perhaps trouble a woman"? his word of the "readiness"—ready for what? his playing with the idea of what is "to come"—what is it? and his final resignation: "Since no man has ought of what he leaves—what is't to leave betimes"? Why should a young man think of dying when he prepares himself for a fencing-match that is nothing but a fencing-match? Or the other way round: if Hamlet speaks of the possibility of meeting his death can he at the same time think he is going to have a mere "sword-play"? The only conclusion is obvious: Hamlet knows full well that in the ensuing "fencing-match" he will have to fight for his life.

*

So far, only the workings of Hamlet's mind and his own words have been considered. He is "ready" to say farewell. Why not let "it come now"? Why not "leave betimes"? But is it "betimes"? Is the situation for him such that, rather than "to grunt and sweat under a weary life", he would prefer death?

In I. 2 ("O, that this too, too solid flesh would melt . . .") he was still unaware of his father's murder; nor did he know anything yet of his mother's adultery; he was only disgusted at the "dexterity" of her second marriage. And yet even then he would have committed suicide had not the Everlasting fixed

> His canon 'gainst self-slaughter.

When he speaks of "To be or not to be" he carries with him the burden of the Ghost's story, but he does not know yet whether those accusations are true. Yet here, convinced as he now is of the King's crime and his mother's adultery, should we not expect his weariness of life to have returned with renewed and increased force?

His longing for that "consummation devoutly to be wish'd" has been held back as long as there was still hope for him to fulfil his father's command. But now? Not only is the task still as impossible as at the beginning; the situation has even worsened for at least two reasons: Claudius knows now that his crime has been discovered and is, accordingly, more on his guard than before (he even seeks to destroy his enemy) and Hamlet has now another deadly foe, Laertes. So he "embraces freely" what under the disguise of a "fencing-match" is offered him: the end.

*

Here, however, two questions call for answers. First:

if Hamlet resigns his life by giving his enemies the chance
of destroying him under the pretext of a sword-play, why
does he not say so openly? Did he not on the previous
occasions speak frankly enough of his suicidal tendencies?
But those two occasions were soliloquies: he was thinking
only, and merely by the miracle called "stage-convention"
were his thoughts audible. In the presence of others he
would not talk of "self-slaughter", especially not in the
presence of so good a friend as Horatio is.

The other question is: if he despairs of ever being able
to avenge his father and if, instead of dragging out a
hateful life, he longs to be rid of it, why does he not kill
himself rather than permit others to kill him?

There are probably various answers: religious scruples,
considerations of personal pride, and other reasons. The
chief reason, however, seems to be that, as long as
Gertrude is alive, his hands are bound. The regard for his
mother's reputation makes it impossible for him to proceed
against her husband; and it makes it likewise impossible
for him to proceed against himself. Not only would he
rob her of her only son; his voluntary death would amount
to an open indictment: the world would accuse her of
having caused his suicide by her "incestuous" marriage,
perhaps suspect her of more. His death would mean
punishment for her, grief, and humiliation, at least in her
own conscience. Yet his father had expressly directed
him:

. . . leave her to heaven . . .

—and when he had tried to deviate from that command
the Ghost had interfered in person. Thus "cabin'd, cribb'd,
confin'd, bound in'', he gladly welcomes the door into the
open, the possibility of "leaving betimes" under the
pretext of being killed in a "fencing-match".

True, by taking that path he would fail to avenge the

murder; but he would at least comply with the Ghost's second request: to spare Gertrude. And this second point seems of greater importance—at least now—to both of them, father as well as son. Love, it seems, weighs more heavily in the end than revenge.

*

Finally, before turning to the last scene, there is yet another subject that calls for some investigation: Who is Osric?

He is usually played as a nincompoop, and his puffed-up language and circumlocutionary verbosity are doubtless comic. Still, it seems to me that to take him as comic and nothing else would be mistaken. His function is similar to that of the "rural fellow" in *Antony and Cleopatra* who in the last act delivers the deadly serpents. He is called a "Clown" and his speech and manner of speaking is clownish enough. Yet who would think of him as nothing but a comic figure?* Nor can the Button-moulder in *Peer Gynt* be taken as a mere mechanic. There are in fact many disguises for the Angel of Death.

Osric is a dark angel. It can hardly be doubted that he knows of the murder plot or even actively helps in it. It is he whom Claudius addresses:

Give them the foils, young Osric

—and again it is he to whom the dying Laertes says that he is caught in his own "springe":

I am justly killed with mine own treachery

—which all tends to show that Osric is an accomplice. And it is evidently his bad conscience that makes him

* *See* Appendix, *Note G.*

talk in the way he does, trying to hide his real intentions behind high-flown verbiage and a frozen grin of forced friendliness. If the actor has the power of auto-suggestion to make himself feel that he is talking so amiably to a man who within half an hour will be dead, killed with his own, Osric's, active help, I have no doubt that the macabre impression Shakespeare evidently wishes to create will be brought out.

Now, Hamlet who suspects his uncle even before the message from beyond reaches him; who suspects Rosencrantz and Guildenstern as spies; who suspects Ophelia as a decoy; who suspects the King's letter—would the same Hamlet, with his truly "prophetic soul", fail to suspect Osric?

But, it may be objected, does not Hamlet merely poke fun at that "waterfly"? It is, to begin with, rather bitter fun; the jests and quibbles Hamlet hurls at him are cruel, sharp, almost slashing. Still, although he treats Osric scathingly enough, would he, if suspecting foul play, be in the mood to make fun of the same man who invites him to the play? Yet we have seen, only a quarter of an hour before, that Hamlet is not overawed by the thought, or even so to speak by the presence, of death. The way he treats the various skulls in the graveyard is not at all respectful. Why should he feel more respect for a skull merely because it is still on its owner's neck? But it is immediately after the possessor of that particularly "fine pate full of fine dirt" has left him that he exclaims:

But thou would'st not think how all here about my heart—but it is no matter.*

*

* *See* Appendix, *Note H*.

XIII

The "Reconcilement"

How does the suggestion just proffered of Hamlet's attitude—the suggestion that he is aware of the dangerous nature of the invitation, but is prepared to make the "fencing-match", if need be, his final exit—how does it square with the proceedings of the last scene?

There is first the question of Hamlet's reconciliation with Laertes. Hamlet cannot possibly suspect any danger in the sword-play if, before this begins, he shakes hands with his enemy, thus making up their quarrel. But —and that is my counter-question—does he really do so? Is there really any reconciliation between him and Laertes?

Opening the "accepted" text at the beginning of the fencing-scene we find in every edition after the King's line: "Come, Hamlet, come, and take this hand from me." The following stage-direction (or words to the same effect):

*The King puts the hand of Laertes into that of Hamlet.**

Yet neither Quarto 2 nor Folio has any such direction; in either text there is nothing between the King's line and Hamlet's speech, beginning with:

Give me your pardon, sir, I've done you wrong. . . .

And if we look into Quarto 1 to ascertain how the passage reads there, we find the following:

Enter King, Queene, Laertes, Lordes.

* Prof. J. Q. Adams has the direction: "Hamlet seizes the hand of Laertes."

121

King Now sonne *Hamlet*, we haue laid vpon your head,
    And make no question but to haue the best.
Ham. Your maiestie hath laide a the weaker side.
King We doubt it not, deliuer them the foiles.

None of the texts, it appears, shows any trace of that stage-direction. It was Hanmer (1744) who first inserted it. Dr. Johnson (1765) took it up and all subsequent editions followed suit. Thus for two centuries all the readers of *Hamlet* have been led to visualize Hamlet and Laertes shaking hands and, accordingly, to take it that they enter the sword-play as reconciled friends. Nor has there been any stage-production (except the one already mentioned) without that sentimental demonstration of manliness. Surely this is all wrong? Between the two no reconciliation takes place at all.

What I think must be regarded as the real stage-proceedings is that Claudius tries to make them shake hands but does not succeed. Were Laertes willing to forgive Hamlet, or to pretend that he does, the two would shake hands without any words at all, or perhaps with half a dozen words to the effect: "All right, that's settled now." Instead, Hamlet has nineteen lines and Laertes replies with eight. Do they, in those twenty-seven lines, speak of their reconciliation as an accomplished fact? Not at all. Hamlet does not acknowledge having been forgiven; he asks—and goes on asking—to be forgiven.

On the other hand, what does Laertes say? His reply is blunt enough; it comes, paraphrased, to this:

In my nature—yes; although nature demands revenge. As regards my honour, however, I refuse reconciliation until a Court of Chivalry has pronounced judgement. Only for this sword-play I will accept the friendship you offer and return it likewise.

Coming from a man whose intention is murder under the disguise of a play, the answer is appropriately involved and ambiguous; yet the main point, the real reply, is made absolutely clear:

I stand aloof and *will no reconcilement.* . . .

Even in Quarto 1 Laertes's refusal comes out plainly, despite the cruel abridgement of the text, especially in this scene. The decisive words have been retained verbally:

Lear. Sir I am satisfied in nature,
But in termes of honor I'le stand aloofe,
And will no reconcilement,
Till by some elder maisters of our time
I may be satisfied.
King Giue them the foyles.

In all three texts Laertes says, "I . . . will no reconcilement." How can we reconcile that with the alleged reconciliation?

We must disregard that unauthorized stage-direction and follow the text alone; if we do so we arrive at something like this: The King takes Laertes by the hand and draws him towards Hamlet. Laertes, however, not feeling at ease in his new role as assassin, shrinks from that all too shameless pretence of friendship, and takes a step back. When Hamlet has finished his speech, Laertes, divided in his mind between honesty and revenge, performs a contortionist's act: ". . . nature . . . should stir me . . . but . . . honour . . . no reconcilement, till . . . but till that time . . ."—words, words, words; but not the slightest indication of a handshake.

*

But now, what is it Hamlet talks about in his nineteen
lines? His first two lines are perfectly clear:

Give me your pardon, sir, I've done you wrong,
But pardon't as you are a gentleman.

They seem, moreover, to be sufficient in themselves;
everybody, I think, has the feeling that here Hamlet
should stop and wait for his opponent's reply. But he goes
on for another seventeen lines, talking of his own madness.
He does so, we have the impression, in a strange and
strained, somehow unnatural manner. He speaks of
himself in the third person: "If Hamlet . . . not himself
. . . his madness . . .", and so forth. Twice in his
speech, although addressing Laertes, he turns to the
Court: "This presence knows . . ." and: "Sir, in this
audience . . ." All that, at first sight, seems artificial
and superfluous; on second thoughts, however, the
suspicion arises whether there is not some hidden meaning
behind it all. What, in that seemingly overlong speech, is
Hamlet driving at?

Prof. J. Q. Adams takes Hamlet's apology as "spoken
with such obvious sincerity that Laertes is forced to
accept it . . ." and he adds: "putting his arm in a
brotherly way about Laertes' shoulder, he (Hamlet) leads
him over to the table where the foils are arranged."

Granville-Barker maintains that Hamlet's "apology
to Laertes is candid". Having quoted his speech "in its
riddling logic" he puts the question: "Did his aping of
madness send him verily mad?" Then, "the two thus
reconciled," Granville-Barker goes on to describe the
fencing-match itself.

Professor Dover Wilson is of opinion that Hamlet's
speech "is a noble and touching plea for forgiveness and
for affection; to suppose it based upon a subterfuge is
monstrous". It is known that he regards Hamlet if not

as outright mad, at least as tottering on the brink of
madness. "In *Hamlet*," Dover Wilson says, (pp. 218–19)

Shakespeare set out to create a hero labouring under
mental infirmity, just as later in *Macbeth* he depicted a
hero afflicted by moral infirmity, or in *Othello* a hero
tortured by an excessive and morbid jealousy. Hamlet
struggles against his weakness, and the struggle is in
great measure the ground-work of his tragedy. But
though he struggles in vain, and is in the end brought
to disaster, a disaster largely of his own making and
involving his own house and that of Polonius, we are
never allowed to feel that his spirit is vanquished until
"the potent poison quite o'ercrows" it. Had he been
represented as a mere madman, we should of course
have felt this; he would have ceased to be a hero and,
while retaining our pity, would have forfeited our
sympathy, our admiration—and our censure. Ophelia
exclaims,

O, what a noble mind is here o'erthrown!

We know better; we realize that the mind is impaired.

Later (on p. 275) Professor Dover Wilson says that

to question the good faith of his request for pardon and
of his plea of "a sore distraction", as most critics have
done, is to murder a beautiful effect. Shakespeare
intended the speech to win our hearts, and never for a
moment expected us to take it at anything but its face
value. The proof of Hamlet's sincerity is that his later
conduct is consistent with it and that Laertes is
evidently shaken by his generosity. . . .

*

125

My suggestion is that in the main part of that speech Hamlet, though to all appearance addressing Laertes, in reality speaks to his mother; it is she from whom he really requests forgiveness.

When in IV. 3, on being sent to England, he turns to leave he stops for a moment: his thought is with his mother. Will he ever see her again? His words are:

But come, for England. Farewell, dear mother.

These words, as I take them, are sincere and uttered as a true farewell. Claudius throws in his: "Thy loving father, Hamlet"—and only then does Hamlet again spew out his bitterness: ". . . man and wife is one flesh: and so, my mother." At that time he was, at least as far as he knew, in less danger than he is now. Having learned of his uncle's murderous intentions and being on the point of entering the "fencing-match" of which he is aware that the outcome will possibly be his own death, is it not natural that his thought should again turn to his mother? His mother comes in; she is going to witness what may be his departure for that undiscover'd country. Of course he asks himself: is he ever to see her again?

He had not seen her since the Closet-scene. He had had no opportunity to make up for his wild behaviour in that dismal night. He longs to be kind to her and to beg her forgiveness. But in the presence of the King and the whole Court, how can he talk to her? What they had spoken to each other on that occasion is a close secret and must be kept secret for ever. He cannot address her directly. But perhaps he could try, while speaking to Laertes, to speak in such a way that she understands that in reality he is talking to her? A difficult problem. And yet, that is what he actually does.

Nowhere throughout the play is there any talk, i.e., in Hamlet's presence, of his madness, except in the Closet-

scene. There, when he speaks to the Ghost whom she does
not perceive, the Queen exclaims: "Alas, he's mad!"
Whether or not he hears her words makes no difference;
for when the Ghost has gone she returns to the matter,
only that this time she uses the euphemistic expression:
"ecstasy". He takes the word up, but exchanges it at
once for the more accurate term: "madness". Three
times he uses the word, imploring his mother not to
believe that he is actuated by madness. Later he uses the
word a fourth time, asking her not to reveal to the King
the fact that his madness is not genuine, but merely
"made in craft".* (Folio; Quarto 2 has "mad in craft".)
Accordingly he can be certain that the word "madness",
if only stressed and reiterated often enough, will remind
her (as a sort of leit-motiv) of that fateful night when he
had treated her so rudely and menacingly that his father's
ghost had to step in and prevent him from further action.

Standing on the threshold of the other world ("the
readiness is all") and wishing to speak to his mother—
possibly, as he thinks, for the last time—what may he
want to express? Would it not be something like this?

"When I last saw you I was hard to you, even cruel.
You wept, but you endured it all because you thought
I was seized by madness. Yes, I must have been mad,
or I could not have acted as I did. Forgive me. Ascribe
it all to my madness. The ghost existed in my imagination only. My talk to him, my suspicions, my recrimina-
tions, all was sheer madness. I had no purpose to hurt
you; I did so, but inadvertently only—like one who
shoots his arrow over the house."

---

* i.e., "counterfeit." Other instances: *King Lear*, IV. 7. 9: ". . . to be
known shortens my *made* intent" and *I. King Henry IV*, II. 4. 548:
"thou are essentially *made* without seeming so." Probably also *The
Tempest*, I. 2. 425: "if you be *made* or no" (for "maid"). *Vide* Spenser:
"And art with her contending, doth aspire T'excel the natural with
made delights."

This, I suggest, is what he really means to say while he appears still to address Laertes. In the hearing of Claudius and the Court, Hamlet has a private talk with his mother: he apologizes and asks to be forgiven. Twice, under a thin disguise, he turns to her: after "This presence knows" and after "Sir, in this audience" there are significant gaps in the versification, gaps to be filled in by action, i.e., by courteous bows to his mother. (To uphold his role as madman he will presumably execute these bows with a kind of stilted irony or stylized eccentricity; still, for all his emotional camouflage, she will be at one with her son.) She does not reply in words. How could she? But an understanding smile will plainly acknowledge the secret bond, reasserted in the last moment between mother and son: their exchange of forgiveness.

*

By some critics, however, Hamlet's apology has been called undignified, insincere, hypocritical. Dr. Johnson, it seems, was the first to feel that there is something unusual in that speech, something irrational. In his blunt manner he says:

I wish, Hamlet had made some other defence; it is unsuitable to the character of a brave or a good man to shelter himself in falsehood.

If we take the speech as "defence" behind which Hamlet endeavours to exculpate himself, making his "madness" (though it is merely feigned) the excuse for the wrongs he has done, in fact, attempting to wriggle out of his own responsibility, then indeed there is "falsehood". But should my suggestion be accepted, then the speech is a desperate and moving endeavour by Hamlet, despite "this presence" and despite "this audience" (the expression "audience" is particularly conclusive), to communicate with his mother—as desperate and as moving as the attempt of a prisoner to get a message through to the outer world by knocking on the wall of his dungeon.

There stands a son who is not only bound hand and foot, but whose mouth is sealed also. He must despair of ever having a private talk with his mother again; for him, after that "fencing-match", time, he presumes, will probably have stopped. Here, with the King sitting at her side, he cannot speak to her either; for whatever he might say by way of apology for his behaviour in that night scene must rouse her husband's suspicions. And Claudius must never learn that Hamlet has ever maintained he had seen a ghost, and had spoken with him, and that this ghost was his dead father. That secret must be kept from the King, now more than ever; for by now Hamlet has decided, should "it come now" and he lose his life, he would secure the comparative happiness of a mother still alive rather than avenge a father who is a mere ghost. "What is't to leave betimes?" He is prepared to go; but if he must go he wishes to spare her name, to save her from humiliation. This, we may say, is not "unsuitable to the character of a brave or a good man".

*

The final evidence I wish to adduce is the Folio text of the passage. There the last word of the speech is not "brother" as in the Quartos, but "mother".

The Folio version of *Hamlet* is in every respect, in punctuation, verse-division, in its cuts, and other matters so greatly superior to that of Quarto 2, not to speak of Quarto 1, that the Folio reading should always be our first conjecture. In this I am diametrically opposed to Professor Dover Wilson, who in *The Manuscript of*

Shakespeare, Cambridge, 1934, gives preference to the
text of Quarto 2. While translating the play in 1935 I
constantly and carefully consulted that book, with the
result that in each single one of the controversial readings
I returned to the Folio.

In this, the last lines of Hamlet's apology read like
this:

> Sir, in this Audience,
> Let my disclaiming from a purpos'd euill,
> Free me so farre in your most generous thoughts,
> That I haue shot mine Arrow o're the house,
> And hurt my Mother.

Should his speech despite its length fail to convey
Hamlet's meaning, then his last word "mother", accompanied by an expressive glance or gesture, should be
enough to remove all doubts; and a smiling nod on her
part would happily round off that dialogue—a silent, or
half-silent, dialogue—between mother and son, for both
of whom, within a quarter of an hour, the rest will be
silence.

*

It is not Shakespeare's habit, when finishing a play, to
leave loose ends hanging in mid-air. On the contrary, it
may be said that he has a veritable horror of loose ends, so
much so that sometimes—in the comedies—a hastily
summoned Hymen must come to the rescue. In the
tragedies we never find that relations between the main
characters are left unresolved. The only exception seems
to be that of Macbeth and his Lady; yet there it is just
the complete estrangement into which the two have
drifted that Shakespeare wishes to show, demonstrating it
by the fact that in the later part of the play they are never

seen together. As a rule, main characters, before their final exit, be it death or no, are clearly shown in their place and in the state of emotional reciprocity in which the whirlpool of the action has landed them.

That being so, why should it be different in the case of Hamlet and his mother? Gertrude, no doubt, is a main character; she is more important in the fabric of the composition than Laertes, or Ophelia, even more than Claudius. Yet if we take Hamlet's apology "at nothing but its face value", as Professor Dover Wilson wishes us to do, then indeed is one thread of the network, and a vital one, cut in mid-air. Surely we cannot suspect Shakespeare of having left so integral a part of the play unresolved? That consideration too, I should think, speaks in favour of the suggestion that Hamlet's aim in that speech is indeed reconciliation; not so much with Laertes, however, as with his mother.

Still, the question remains: does she really forgive him? Are they really reconciled before they die? They are; I do not doubt it.

In these remaining few minutes of her life Gertrude is happy; happier than we have ever seen her. She is joyful: her son has forgiven her and she has forgiven him. Perhaps all will be well again? And here now, there is a pause in the sword-play, both fencers being tired; now she has a chance to speak to her son, and she makes use of it.

> He's fat, and scant of breath.
> Heere's a Napkin, rub thy browes.

(the text is that of the Folio)—and after "browes" there is a gap in the verse. For what purpose? For Hamlet to come up and take the napkin from her.

Now here the question, at first sight a trifling one, arises: is Hamlet actually perspiring? No doubt he is. But then, would he not, if his brow is wet, use the handkerchief at once? and with his own hand? Of course he does

131

so. For reasons which will be clear in a moment I give here the whole passage (from the Folio):

Qu.   He's fat, and scant of breath.
        Heere's a Napkin, rub thy browes.
        The Queene Carowses to thy fortune, *Hamlet.*
Ham.   Good Madam.
King.   Gertrude, do not drinke.
Qu.   I will my Lord:
        I pray you pardon me.
King.   It is the poyson'd Cup, it is too late.
Ham.   I dare not drinke yet Madam,
        By and by.
Qu.   Come, let me wipe thy face.
Laer.   My Lord, Ile hit him now.
King.   I do not think't.
Laer.   And yet 'tis almost 'gainst my conscience.
Ham.   Come for the third. . . .

Surely we cannot imagine that Hamlet should all this time stand, handkerchief in hand, and not use it? Of course he takes it and at once wipes his brow. It would be ridiculous for him to wait until the Queen has taken and lifted the cup, spoken to Claudius, drunk of the wine, offered the half-empty cup to her son, and replaced it. If that behaviour on Hamlet's part seems improbable then Gertrude's words: "Come, let me wipe thy face" must be a mere subterfuge. And so they are. Gertrude only wishes to show kindness to her son, to fondle him, to be once more his loving mother.

Whether she actually pretends to wipe his face is of no importance. Perhaps she smoothes his hair, perhaps she embraces him, perhaps merely touches his hand. Nor do I venture to suggest definitely what he might do: perhaps he kneels down, perhaps he kisses her hand, perhaps he simply smiles at her, happy to see her happy. Yet whatever the action, this short and (as so often in

Shakespeare) silent scene is—and I do not hesitate to
say so—the climax of the play: it shows the reconciliation
between the guilty mother and her son who, for the sake
of his father's and his own love, forgives her.

*

That Shakespeare found it necessary to talk about
Hamlet's perspiration has occasioned considerable
embarrassment. The words "He's fat" have been the
cause of linguistic as well as æsthetic scruples.* It seems
more than probable that the otherwise so negligible
incident of Hamlet's wet brow was invented by Shakespeare expressly to make it possible for him to bring
mother and son together, thus making their reconciliation clearly visible. In doing so he brings Gertrude away
from her husband's side for a short time so that Claudius
and Laertes may have their "whispered" conversation all
the more audibly:

  Laer.: My lord, I'll hit him now.
  King: I do not think't.
  Laer.: And yet 'tis almost 'gainst my conscience.

Such is Shakespeare's stage-craft: on the one side we
have the plotters speaking their mind, on the other side
mother and son silently united for the last time and in the
last glimpse of happiness, she wiping his face or stroking
his hair, and he . . . but how he reacts to her tenderness,
that, I feel, should be left to the actor.

*

Finally there is the word "madness" that, strikingly
stressed and reiterated as it is, has been the cause of much
controversy. As long as the whole of the speech is taken

* *See* Appendix, *Note I.*

133

as addressed to Laertes there is this dilemma, which indeed seems insoluble: Either Hamlet is mad—but then, how can a madman recognize his own madness and openly speak of it?—or he is not mad—what meanness, then, "to shelter himself in falsehood"?

Professor Dover Wilson asserts that the speech "is the most positive statement of Hamlet's madness by Hamlet himself in the whole play"—and he comes to the following conclusion, which seems to be made of "changeable taffeta":

> Hamlet can draw a line between "himself" and "his madness", a thing impossible for Ophelia; and so we gain the impression that he is usually normal but subject to occasional fits of madness.

Hamlet, when referring to his "madness" does not intend to make a statement; least of all does he wish us, i.e., the audience, to regard what he says as truth. There is only one person whom he desires to accept his speech "at its face value", and that is his mother. If she finds comfort in the thought that only his madness and nothing else made him rage so savagely against her; if it eases her mind to believe that he saw the ghost in his hallucination only—why, is he not ready to sacrifice even his own life? What, then, should make him shrink from a white lie? He is now in the mood of: "It is no matter"; nothing now counts any more; and so he "confesses": yes, it was madness. All he wishes to achieve by telling her so is to set her heart at peace, whatever the hour may bring. It is the son who speaks out of considerateness for his mother, and not a patient who discloses the true conditions of his mental state.

To my mind there is not in the whole play a single occasion when Hamlet even by one step passes beyond the bounds of sanity. /

*

XIV

The "Fencing-Match"

LAERTES of course does not understand the hidden meaning in Hamlet's speech; he answers what he thinks was a request to him. His reply is both Yes and No and therefore neither Yes nor No. He indeed "shelters himself in falsehood". Hamlet cannot have expected any different answer. He recognizes his enemy's reply as what it is: a disguised challenge, disguised merely because the Queen is present. For her sake some pretence of friendship must be kept up. On that point all three of them are agreed, the two assassins and their victim alike.

To imagine Hamlet to be so full of credulity as to expect that Laertes would forgive him truly and genuinely, merely on account of a few dozen words; or even as to believe that Laertes would hold his enmity in suspense for the duration of the sword-play, would be vastly to underrate Hamlet's mental faculties. On board ship he had suspected Rosencrantz and Guildenstern of being the King's instruments, and in fact found out that they had lowered themselves to the point of becoming clandestine executioners; they had accepted that murderous job although he had never done them any wrong. Here on the other hand is Laertes, who burns to avenge his own father's death and whom he, Hamlet, had just before so rudely attacked and coarsely abused over Ophelia's coffin. This same Laertes comes in, led on the leash as it were by him who, Hamlet knows, seeks his life without the slightest scruple. It is Claudius who endeavours to reconcile him with his minion. That too cannot but strengthen his suspicions. And finally, there is Laertes's answer: ". . . nature . . . revenge . . . terms of honour. . . ."

I stand aloof and will no reconcilement,
Till by some elder masters. . . .

To take it that on top of that mountain of gross
suspicions Hamlet should stand like a guileless child,
innocently assuming that neither Claudius nor Laertes
mean to do him the smallest harm, goes, I think, beyond
credibility.

My own suggestion has been set forth already; it is,
that Hamlet knows perfectly well that he will have to
fight for his life; that he is determined to sell his life as
dearly as possible; and that for his mother's sake he
accepts, and himself upholds, the pretence of a sword-play.

It now remains to examine whether that suggestion is
consistent with text and proceedings of the fencing-scene.

*

First, familiar as we are with Hamlet's scornful way
of talking, should we not expect him to make it known to
Laertes, if only with a few words of subtle allusion, that
he sees through the foul play? That is what he actually
does; the text seems to show that plainly enough.

(a) Laertes says (in the Folio):

I do receiue your offer'd loue like loue,
And wil not wrong it.

—whereupon Hamlet replies:

I do embrace it freely,
And will this Brothers wager frankely play.

The following quotations show that Shakespeare is
wont to use the verb "to embrace" in connection with
death.

Macbeth. III, 1. 137:

> Fleance, his son . . . must embrace the fate
> Of that dark hour.

The Two Gentlemen of Verona, V. 4. 126:

> Thurio, give back, or else embrace thy death.

All's Well That Ends Well, III. 4. 17:

> He is too good and fair for Death and me,
> Whom I myself embrace to set him free.

The adverb "freely", instead of which we should expect something like "gladly", seems to go better with a sterner embrace than that of love. But Laertes does not offer love at all; he merely consents to "receive" Hamlet's "love", and assures him of one thing only: that he will not wrong Hamlet's love. The "it" which Hamlet is prepared to embrace hangs somewhat in the air, both in grammar and sense.

Also the adverb "frankly" seems to go better with a real fight than with a mere play. Whether "Brothers wager" is one brother's or two brothers' wager no one can say; Quarto 2 has "brothers wager", and Quarto 1 omits the passage altogether. Thus it is uncertain whether the wager is one of Ophelia's brother or a wager between brothers.

(*b*) The combatants call for the foils. "Come on" and "Come, one for me". Still, Hamlet continues sneering:

> I'll be your foil, Laertes, in mine ignorance
> Your skill shall like a star i'the darkest night
> Stick fiery off indeed.

The pun, playing with the double sense of "foil", is

obvious. What, however, is "mine ignorance"? If Hamlet wishes to say that he is a bad fencer or in poor form he has chosen an inadequate expression. "Ignorance" for "lack of practice" is, as far as I know, nowhere else to be found in Shakespeare. But perhaps the meaning Hamlet wants to convey is something like: "You don't think I am ignorant of the true situation, do you?" There is yet another grim pun: "to stick off" means "to stand out from the surface", but also "to stab, to kill off".

(c) Laertes apparently understands Hamlet's scorn quite well; he says: "You mock me, sir." Hamlet answers:

No, by this hand.

Is this merely an asseveration, like "By this light" or similar rather meaningless exclamations, or does it contain more?

In *The Tempest*, III. 2. 57, we have the following:

Trinculo, if you trouble him any more in his tale, by this hand, I will supplant some of your teeth.

—which shows that "by this hand" may also be used as a threat.

(d) The King asks Hamlet whether he knows the wager; he receives the answer:

Very well, my lord,
Your grace hath laid the odds a'th' weaker side.

Hamlet knows his uncle's intentions. This time he does not say: "I see a Cherub that sees them"; but the two words: "very—well—", appropriately stressed and accompanied by a piercing look, would betray just as much of his emotions as in his mother's presence he is free to express.

Read as I think it should be read, the whole passage appears to be full of the bitterest irony, showing that

138

Hamlet knows the thunderstorm that is brewing, though he cannot know when and how it will break. Of course, as long as Gertrude listens to what he says his words cannot be other than ambiguous. And I have tried to show that in fact they are ambiguous and permit of being spoken by Hamlet in such a way as to impart to his enemies that there are not two but three who are in the know. To bring out that meaning, the actor needs only to declaim the pregnant words as though they stood between inverted commas, slightly colouring them with derision.

*

In IV. 7. 135 ff, when the two are plotting the murder, Claudius assures Laertes that in his opinion Hamlet would be very careless:

> . . . he, being remiss,
> Most generous and free from all contriving,
> Will not peruse the foils, so that with ease
> Or with a little shuffling you may choose
> A sword unbated, and in a pass of practice
> Requite him for your father.

This passage is the source for the general belief that Hamlet, during the main part of the "fencing-match", is "in good faith". But the question must be asked: are the King's words a cheque that Hamlet is obliged to honour?

Throughout the play we regard Claudius as what he is, a criminal. But when he says Hamlet "will not peruse the foils", are we to take his prophecy for gospel?* Besides: is Hamlet really "most generous"? Yes, towards the players, but certainly not towards Rosencrantz and Guildenstern, or Ophelia, or even Polonius. The same man who thinks it sport

---

* Prof. Allardyce Nicoll quotes the first three of the lines given above and says: "This indeed seems an accurate summing-up of his (Hamlet's) nature."

to have the enginer
Hoist with his own petar . . . O, 'tis sweet
When in one line two crafts directly meet. . . .

—he who rifles his fellow-travellers' baggage: can he really be called "free from all contriving"? Not even what Claudius praises in his nephew can be taken as true; still less can we believe that Hamlet is as careless, criminally careless, as at that moment it suits Claudius to depict him. At that moment the King wishes to hire an assassin: of course if he endeavours to talk Laertes into accepting that treacherous job he must describe it as simple and free from danger. He even goes so far as to praise Hamlet: all that in the desire to evade the critical point, the peril, with all the greater plausibility. Yet if Laertes in his thirst for revenge is taken in with this deceit, we, being less enraged, should not allow ourselves to be diverted from facts and probabilities by what Claudius, in pursuit of his perfidious aim, says to his dupe Laertes.

*

Surely it is impossible to believe in Hamlet's abysmal carelessness? It seems utterly incredible that a man, surrounded by treason, murder, revenge, as Hamlet knows he is, should not take every imaginable precaution. He knows that both his enemies are intent on destroying him. And now, when they bring in their weapons—rapiers and daggers—when they measure the foils, when Laertes lifts his rapier in formal salutation, when they start fencing: is it conceivable that all this time Hamlet should not cast one glance at his opponent's weapon and its point?

In the text there is at first sight no direct evidence that could be referred to in favour of this conception; but a strong proof seems to lie in what is missing in the text, i.e., any indication of surprise on Hamlet's part when he is wounded. Were he actually "in good faith", namely believing all along that he is engaged in a mere sword-play, of course, when he receives his wound, we should expect him to exclaim: "Hah—how is this?"—or something to that effect.* Yet when after several bouts Laertes calls out: "Have at you now!" and lands his thrust, drawing blood from his opponent, not a single word comes from Hamlet's lips.

In the Folio there is merely the stage-direction:

In scuffling they change Rapiers.

Quarto 2 has nothing about the exchange of the weapons; there the text continues uninterruptedly:

Laer.   Haue at you now.
King.   Part them, they are incenst.
Ham.   Nay come againe.

—and Quarto 1 has this:

*They catch one anothers Rapiers, and both are wounded,
Leartes falles downe, the Queene falles downe and dies.*

Much ink has been spilt in explaining the intricacies of the fencing act itself, of how the two come one by the other's rapier, and so forth.† Yet the primary question is and should be: how is it that Hamlet does not express surprise? There can, I think, be only one answer: because he is not surprised. It is consistent both with the text and the whole situation to take it that Hamlet knows from the beginning that the rapier in Laertes's hand is unbated. Yet even should his eye be less sharp than his suspicion

* *See* Appendix, *Note J*.
† *See* Appendix, *Note K*.

he would, when wounded, be surprised only at the means employed by the traitors and not at the treachery itself. A moment's pause and a contemptuous smile round his lips, expressing: "Aha, so this is your trick!"—would be all his reaction before he continues the fight, first of all taking the pointed rapier from his enemy's hand.

Added, however, to that negative evidence, lying in the absence of surprise, there seems after all to be one piece of definitely positive evidence. When Laertes discloses that the treacherous weapon is not only pointed but also poisoned, Hamlet expresses his astonishment at the second matter only:

> The point envenomed too?

What surprises him is not that a sharp rapier has been used, but that, in addition, it has been poisoned.

*

Both opponents are bleeding. The Queen is on the point of dying. Claudius, in a last sauve-qui-peut, tries to save his own life. When Laertes calls out: "How does the Queen?" the King answers with the lie:

> She swounds to see them bleed.

Once more the over-crafty criminal blunders and defeats himself by going just one step too far. He thinks it very clever to give the explanation that the Queen is merely fainting; and just by that one step he brings immediate catastrophe on his own head. Hearing his lie and feeling her end to be near, Gertrude definitely frees herself from her husband; in this last minute she severs the bond between them and takes refuge with her son. And in that way it should, I think, be played: gathering her last strength she breaks away from Claudius, crosses

over to Hamlet, as though she wished to speak to him,
and collapses in his arms.

Had not her tongue failed her, what would she have
told her son? With Death already stretching his hand
towards her, all restraints have gone, all consideration for
the seducer who committed murder in order to marry her.
Now she could speak "as liberal as the north"; now she
could at last reveal what really happened, and even
divulge her own share in it—and it seems she wishes to do
so. But the hand of Death closes her lips.

Yet although she takes her secret with her to the tomb,
Gertrude's death changes the situation immediately and
fundamentally. The moment she departs the invisible
fetters fall from her son's hands: he is—at last!—free to
act. That insoluble problem no longer exists: the double
task (revenge, yet nothing against Gertrude) has suddenly
been reduced to the single task of dispatching the murderer.
Now indeed the whole business is most simple and easy: it
consists in nothing more than in running a rapier through
the smiling villain—and that Hamlet settles at once and
most efficiently.

What now remains of the accusations levelled against
Hamlet of inactivity, of irresolution, of weakness of
character, of the ruin of a high soul by over-cultivation
of the mind, or whatever else he is blamed for? As long
as he is saddled with a task impossible of fulfilment he
cannot act. No one could have acted. Not even Hercules
in person could have taken revenge and at the same time
spared Gertrude. But as soon as Claudius himself removes
that obstacle, i.e., Gertrude's life (who, while alive, had
shielded her husband) there is no Hercules needed to
execute the remainder of the task. Hamlet himself does
all that is demanded and does it at once, without hesitation, procrastination or scruple.

Such is the functioning of Shakespeare's whirligig of

143

time. It lies in Hamlet's character that he takes that
jump ahead of the others, thus becoming the only prisoner
of the pirates: and it is due to that jump that he returns
to Denmark. It lies in Claudius's character that he takes
that one step too far, thus, with his "union", killing
Gertrude: and it is due to Gertrude's death that Hamlet is
free to act. Had not Claudius, overdoing his craftiness,
poisoned the Queen, Hamlet would have died of the
"envenomed" rapier, and not only Gertrude but Claudius,
too, would have survived him: so near does the murderer
come to escaping scot-free. And yet, it is he himself who,
because he is just a little too clever, puts his head into the
noose.

There is nothing left to chance. Everyone acts as he or
she must, according to the mechanism of their minds.
Everything that happens or fails to happen is founded on
character or is the outcome of that conflict of characters
which after all is the quintessence of drama. The fact that
by this conflict of characters the action so fashions itself
that in the end, almost in the last minute, already dying,
Hamlet is allowed to avenge his father's death, is proof
indeed that

> There's a divinity that shapes our ends,
> Rough-hew them how we will.

Whether this divinity is Shakespeare's own or whether
it refers, as Shakespeare himself means it to do, to another
still higher power makes no real difference: source and
result are the same.

*

XV

The Rock in the River

Before proceeding to the last chapter I have to return to the central part of the play; my reasons for doing so will be apparent very soon.

Most critics have noticed the phenomenon that the Hamlet who returns to Denmark differs from the Hamlet we have known before. "When he emerges safe from the ambush of his voyage," Granville-Barker says, "we are to know, by the wistfully humorous detachment of his mood, that the fever in his brain is now burnt out."

Professor Dover Wilson, too, regards the returned Hamlet as "a changed man with an air of self-possession greater than at any time of the play". And he goes on:

We are not told why; but we may fancy, if we like, that the seas have helped to expel the "something-settled matter in his heart", or that he has gained confidence from the hoisting of Rosencrantz and Guildenstern with their own petar, or that simply his "cause of distemper" is wearing off. The real cause of the change is, of course, a technical one. The requirements of tragic drama compel his creator to win back our respect for him before the end, to dissipate the clouds at sunset.

Whether it is true that an author can for whatever technical requirement bring about a change in his hero, particularly in the last act, and whether Shakespeare has ever done so, and done so with Hamlet, seems to be rather doubtful. Yet however this may be, the change itself is unmistakable, and the question is: what may have caused that alteration?

If we exclude, as I think we must, any "technical" reason we have to look round for events that may have effected that transformation. Can we believe that the salt breezes have done Hamlet so much good that he comes back a different man? But surely atmospheric interferences of that kind cannot be accepted as motives in a Shakespeare tragedy? Nor can I think that Hamlet was ever lacking in self-confidence; there is no need for him to increase it, least of all by the death of Rosencrantz and Guildenstern. And as to his madness: an author such as Shakespeare creates his hero's mental state and does not wait until the chance of a sea-trip does away with a fit of madness. We must, I feel, look for stronger influences, for deeper reasons.

If we examine Hamlet's development, retracing not so much his sea-voyage as his mental voyage; if we search the dramatic story for that single event that alters with an almost sudden twist his attitude towards Gertrude (for it is the attitude towards his mother in which that change really consists) we find ourselves back in the Closet-scene. There stands the rock that deflects the river of Hamlet's activity so completely—or diverts it, one might say, as though it were the River Alph,

> Through caverns measureless to men
> Down to a sunless sea.

—until in the last scene, the moment Gertrude is dead, the subterranean stream breaks forth in an irresistible torrent.

That rock is the Ghost.

*

In the Commentary added to his edition of the play Prof. Adams gives us an excellent exposition of the change brought about by the Ghost's appearance in the Closet-scene. First, he makes the somewhat startling remark that that appearance

146

has no influence on the course of action. So far as subsequent events are concerned this second interview with Hamlet might be entirely dispensed with—as it often is in modern productions of the play.*

By "subsequent events" Adams apparently means positive actions and occurrences. But if owing to a certain cause an action is omitted or an occurrence avoided, must not the fact that this or that does not materialize also be called an event? Especially in a play in which delay, postponement, frustration are factors at least as important as positive actions? In fact, the psychological change Prof. Adams describes is, it seems to me, the most important event in the whole play. That change is identical with the turn in Hamlet's mental voyage, as I have just called it. "Clearly," Prof. Adams says shortly afterwards,

the scene breaks in the middle; up to the appearance of the Ghost, Hamlet is one sort of man, after that appearance, he is a different sort of man. . . . And, in similar fashion, *the whole play breaks here*; for, as we have said, the coming of the Ghost marks the climax of the plot—the turning-point of the hero's melancholia.

Adams speaks of Hamlet's changed attitude toward his mother, his entirely different mood: "the scene now becomes one of tenderness."

In these observations, it is evident, the deflection both in Hamlet's mentality and in the current of the play is fully recognized, and it is recognized as the effect of the Ghost's appearance. Still, the question, so far unanswered, remains: what is the cause of that so highly conspicuous change? By what means is it produced? Surely the assumption is justified that psychological effects are brought about by psychological motives?

*

* Indeed? "Oh horrible, Oh horrible, most horrible"!

In Chapter VI, I have tried to answer the question why the Ghost appears and interferes in the Closet-scene. His purpose, it seems to me, is not to prevent Hamlet from telling his mother "that her lover and husband is her husband's murderer", but to prevent his son from forcing his mother to confess her share in the crime. This the Ghost achieves by his mere appearance: he interrupts the torrent of Hamlet's invective and thus saves Gertrude from a breakdown in which she would have divulged the extent of her guilt.

That done, however, he does more—and the difficulty to find out what he does lies in the fact that he does it in silence. We hear only from Hamlet's lips that the Ghost is doing something. What is it? The passage reads in the Folio (Quarto 2 differs in punctuation only):

Queen. . . . Whereon do you look?

Ham. On him, on him: look you how pale he glares!
His form and cause conjoin'd, preaching to
stones,
Would make them capable. Do not look upon
me;
Lest with this piteous action you convert
My stern effects: then what I have to do
Will want true colour; tears perchance for
blood——

Queen. To who do you speak this?

Gertrude's last question shows that the latter part of Hamlet's speech is addressed not to her but to the Ghost, whom she neither sees nor hears. What is it Hamlet speaks about? Something he sees the Ghost do; it is "this piteous action". This action, Hamlet is afraid, might have the result of "converting" his "stern effects". What does that action consist in?

Bradley does not refer to it at all; nor does J. Q. Adams. In Granville-Barker's description and explanation of

148

the scene no reference to that "action" is made either. He quotes the apparition's words (pp. 115 ff):

Do not forget. . . .

—a pale, inverted echo of that parting, commanding "Remember me", and the pitiful

But look! amazement on thy mother sits;
O! step between her and her fighting soul! . . .

—for he divines a grace in her, as Hamlet does not, as she herself, it may be, does not yet. Then, after a little, a silent stealing away. It is as if, with the passing of time, the spirit had lost material power, was nearer to its rest and to oblivion.

Later (p. 324) Granville-Barker speaks of the Ghost

enjoying a fleeting happiness with wife and son. Commands to vengeance have become "this piteous action"; the majestic, memorable farewell turns to a stealing away out at the portal.

Professor Dover Wilson quotes Hamlet's words: "On him! on him! . . ." (lines which he calls "as yet unexplained") and explains them as follows:

Hamlet's words indicate some strange agitation in the Ghost's face and actions, an agitation that wrings the son's heart with pity and forces tears to his eyes. What is it? The evidence of the *Brudermord* seems to leave no doubt of the answer. The Queen's words to Hamlet reveal to the Ghost that she is cut off from him, that she can neither hear nor see him; he holds out hands in supplication towards her; he turns a face full of anguish upon Hamlet; and, as the horror of the whole situation dawns upon him and he realizes the reason of her insensibility, he "steals away" in shame, "out at the

portal". It is the last glimpse of King Hamlet; he
returns to his purgatory with the added torment that
he is separated for all eternity from the being he loves
best.

With this interpretation I cannot agree. Why for his
kindheartedness King Hamlet should be punished with
"added torment" is inconceivable. It is true that the
Ghost "steals away"; but the addition of the words "in
shame" is arbitrary. That "he holds out hands in supplication", that he "turns a full face of anguish upon Hamlet"
are details without any foundation in the text. Besides,
it seems impossible to assume that the Ghost does not
know beforehand that he will be invisible and inaudible to
Gertrude; or he would not speak of her, in her presence, in
the manner he does. Also it would be rather late in the
day for him to realize "the reason of her insensibility". In
Professor Dover Wilson's opinion Gertrude is innocent of
any complicity in the murder and guilty merely of
adultery. How, then, can it be that the Ghost only now
"realizes the reason of her insensibility" (this being her
faithlessness) when as early as in I. 5 he has told his son
of her adultery?

Finally, Professor Dover Wilson understands Hamlet's
words as indicating

> some strange agitation in the Ghost's face and actions,
> an agitation that wrings the son's heart with pity and
> forces tears to his eyes.

He evidently takes "piteous action" as an action that
evokes pity ("wrings the son's heart with pity"). In this he
has been anticipated by Schlegel, who translates the words
as "klägliche Gebärde", i.e., "doleful gesture."* Yet it

* Wieland, the first translator of the play into German, had equally
misconstrued the passage; his version, retranslated, reads: "Oh, do not
glance at me, lest this sad look transform my more pious intention into
rage—and make blood flow instead of tears."

seems that a closer examination of the passage does not
bear out that interpretation.

In II. I. 82 Ophelia describes Hamlet's look as "piteous
in purport", meaning that she had to pity him for his
look. Yet in *The Tempest*, I. 2. 14 Prospero, talking to
Miranda, speaks of "your piteous heart", i.e., a heart that
feels pity. In *Richard II*, V. 3. 126 we have "thy piteous
heart", used with the same meaning. In *Venus and
Adonis*, 504, we find "piteous lips", i.e., "lips full of pity,"
in *The Rape of Lucrece*, 1502, "piteous looks," i.e.,
"looks showing pity," and so forth.

Corroborative instances may be found in Spenser. In
The Faerie Queene, II. 10, 44, he speaks of "pitteous
Elidure"; the context shows the meaning to be "feeling
pity". In *Virgils Gnat* we have: "Where the reward of my
so piteous deed?", where "piteous deed" stands for "deed
of pity". In *An Hymne of Heavenly Love* the poet,
describing the Crucifixion, speaks of "the piteous hart Of
that deare Lord".

Milton in his version of Psalm CXXXVI, referring to the
Deity, says:

> He hath with a piteous eye
> Beheld us in our misery.

In his Ode *In Remembrance of Master William
Shakespire* (sic!) D'Avenant warns the poets not to tread
the banks of the mourning Avon: "The piteous river wept
itself away. . . ."

Also the opposite of "piteous" occurs in Shakespeare.
In *Hamlet*, IV, 5, 100, the Messenger says:

> The Ocean (ouer-peering of his List)
> Eats not the Flats with more impittious haste
> Then young *Laertes*. . . .

The *Shorter Oxford English Dictionary* ignores the instance and dates the word "impiteous" ("pitiless") from 1877; it has on the other hand "impittious haste SHAKS", but gives it under "impetuous". In fact, all modern editions print the word as "impetuous", which I think is wrong. In the Folio the word is spelt: "impittious", in Quarto 2: "impitious". (In Quarto 1 it does not appear.) "Piteous" (in "piteous action") is spelt in the Folio as "pitteous", in Quarto 2 as "pittious". I feel convinced that "impittious" of "impitious" is not "impetuous" but "impiteous" haste, meaning "pitiless".

Another term for "lacking pity" is "dispiteous". In Shakespeare it appears in *King John*, IV. I. 34 as "dispitious" ("dispitious torture"); here, too, the *S.O.E.D.* ignores the instance and dates "dispiteous" from 1803. It gives the quotation from *King John*, but under "despiteous" and paraphrases it as "spiteful". Spenser, however, shows clearly that the word means "pitiless". In *The Faerie Queene*, I. 2. 15, we have "rage dispiteous"; in IV. 8. 42, "despiteous dreare"; in II. 6. 29: "steele despiteously entayld," and in II. 7. 62: "to Jewes despiteous Delivered up the Lord."

All that leaves me with little doubt that "piteous action" has to be taken as "action showing pity".

What, on the other hand, is the meaning of the "stern effects" of which Hamlet speaks? It seems that in this connection the word "effect" stands for "purpose". In *Hamlet* itself we find parallels: I. 3. 45: "th' effect of this good lesson"; III. 3. 54: "still possess'd Of those effects for which I did the murder"; V. 2. 37: "The effect of what I wrote." Similar instances may be found in *Macbeth*, I. 5. 76, in *Othello*, I. 3. 105, and in *The Two Gentlemen of Verona*, II. 7. 73.

Accordingly the passage in question may, I think, be paraphrased like this:

"His outer appearance and his cause would impress even stones.—Do not look upon me, or by your action of pity you might divert me from my stern purpose; in this case the fulfilment of my duty will not have the proper result: possibly tears instead of blood. . . ."*

And from this translation as it were we arrive at the following interpretation: What Hamlet perceives is an action (a gesture) expressing pity. Pity for whom? Not for Hamlet of course, but for Gertrude. This show of pity is so moving that Hamlet is afraid it might deflect him from his stern purpose. This purpose can only be that of revenge, which, if the Ghost continues to work on his feelings, will misfire, and the whole enterprise will result not in blood, as it should, but in tears.

Now, however, comes the question: what is that action of pity as far as gesture or other outward show is concerned? I cannot give an answer. Whether the Ghost holds out his hands (certainly not "in supplication towards Gertrude") or whether he makes a sign as if blessing her or whether he folds his hands, silently imploring Hamlet to forgo his cruelty against her, it would be presumptuous in me to suggest. The text simply does not allow of any such detailed interpretation. Yet the general interpretation, its inner contents, seems to me clear beyond any doubt, namely that that "piteous action" indicates the Ghost's forgiveness.

This forgiveness, King Hamlet's silent reconciliation with Gertrude, is the turning-point in the play; for it is the turning-point in Hamlet's behaviour, in his attitude towards his duty. Up to that moment Hamlet had been doing his best to pursue revenge; he had done so in his own way, which is the way of cautiousness and conscientiousness. First he had striven to be convinced

---

* In my own translation of the play I have rendered "this piteous action" with: "deines Mitleids Regung."

of the truthfulness of the Ghost's story. In that he had been successful: he had found the proof in the result of that truly miraculous, because the only possible, scheme, that of the Mouse-trap. Then, his doubts on that point removed, he had proceeded to deal with the other category of his doubts, his suspicions about Gertrude's share in the crime. In this now he finds himself balked by the Ghost's interference. Not only are his endeavours to disclose his mother's guilt frustrated, the Ghost goes even so far as to show pity for her. That, as Hamlet foresees, must paralyse him.

How could it have been otherwise? If the Ghost, the deceived, wronged, and finally murdered husband, shows pity towards his wife, that is to say, if he forgives her—he, the victim—what is there left for his son to do?

*

If the two words: "piteous action" really mean what I take them to mean, then indeed they contain the very core of the play. If that "piteous action" is an "action of pity", weakening Hamlet's purpose of revenge and resulting in tears instead of blood, then that passage is the psychological cross-roads: Hamlet is deflected from his path, both in pursuit of his duty and in his attitude towards his mother.

So far I have based my suggestion on the text as given in Quarto 2 and the Folio. Now, opening Quarto 1, we find what I cannot help feeling is a complete confirmation of the paraphrase offered above.

The text of the passage as given in Quarto 1 shows, I think, clearly that at least this particular passage was "reported" by a player (hardly the actor who took the part of Hamlet) who was unable to remember the exact words, but, having heard the play acted often enough, was in a position to reproduce their main trend not too badly. The resulting lines paraphrase the original passage in a prosaic, though versified, manner. The words, no doubt, are unauthentic; yet their content is certainly a reliable indication as to the meaning of the authentic text.

The parts of Hamlet's speech are shortened and contracted into nine uninterrupted lines:

Enter the ghost in his night gowne.

Saue me, saue me, you gratious
Powers aboue, and houer ouer mee,
With your celestiall wings.
Doe you not come your tardy sonne to chide,
That I thus long haue let reuenge slippe by?
O do not glare with looks so pittifull!
Lest that my heart of stone yeelde to compassion,
And euery part that should assist reuenge,
Forgoe their proper powers, and fall to pitty.

In these words Hamlet addresses his father, asking him not to glare with "looks so pitiful" (i.e., full of pity) lest his "heart of stone" (a heart bent on cruel revenge) may yield to compassion (for his mother, of course) and, foregoing its purpose, "fall to pity" (for Gertrude).

Whichever text we take, the meaning is the same. What Hamlet speaks about, as though he were afraid of it, happens: he cannot but follow the Ghost's example: he "falls to pity" his mother and forgives her.

XVI

Failure or Triumph

It is probably not by chance that King Hamlet and Prince Hamlet bear the same name. The Prince is very much his father's son. We deduce that first from his mourning for him, from his eulogy on him, and other indications of his feelings. We notice it also by the complete understanding between the two, by the readiness with which the son falls in with his father's intentions and, more than anything else, by the ease with which he is persuaded to drop his cruel proceeding against his mother.

Ghosts, i.e., Shakespeare's ghosts, have power only over those to whom they are akin in blood, or from whom they receive life by a kind of blood-transfusion. The ghosts seen by Richard Crookback are the creations of his guilt-oppressed brain. Brutus sees the Ghost of Cæsar because he is still afraid of him and his cause. The Weird Sisters establish their dominance over Macbeth because what they give him—the hope of being king—has already been produced by himself in his dreams of ambition. (Banquo's Ghost is of a different kind; he is an apparition conjured up by the witches in the same way as the various apparitions they produce from their cauldron.) Shakespeare's ghosts are theatrical ectoplasm produced to make visible an otherwise invisible inner strife. The dagger Macbeth is unable to clutch is of that nature: the outward manifestation of an inner conflict.

But conflict there must be. Nothing is permitted to exist on the stage, whether the apparition of a dagger or a person, that does not owe its existence to emotions, tendencies, politics, clashing with each other. Conflict is the life of drama and the only justification for the dramatis personæ, living creatures or ghosts alike.

156

That, I think, explains why after the Closet-scene the Ghost disappears from the play altogether. No points of disagreement are left between father and son. The Ghost is reconciled with Gertrude. In her presence, although she does neither see nor hear him, he has prevailed on their son to forgive her also. There is no longer any difference between the two Hamlets—not merely in the sense that they have ceased to differ, but also in the sense that in aim and function the father has merged in the son. The ectoplasm is swallowed back again by him who had produced it. "Produced it?" Yes, in a sense Hamlet produces the Ghost; every son does so, reproducing the deceased parent at least in memory. Hamlet does so with his "prophetic soul", by his sense of justice, by his weakness as regards Gertrude. Were not the two so completely one, the Ghost could not have worked on his son and the son could not have reproduced and represented his father's cause. His father's spirit is alive in him. And what is the Ghost if not the personification of that spirit?

*

Professor Dover Wilson maintains (p. 268) that Shakespeare "never lets us forget that he (Hamlet) is a failure, or that he has failed through weakness of character". In the preceding chapters I have tried to show that there is no justification whatsoever for calling Hamlet a failure. We might just as well accuse Prometheus, chained to Mount Caucasus, of inactivity and weakness of character. But if we wish to do justice to the play we should never forget that Hamlet himself is not the whole play. *Hamlet* with the Prince of Denmark left out is not the right thing; but just as little is the play thinkable with the Ghost omitted. We have to look at the question of failure from a standpoint where the outline of the play as a whole can be viewed.

157

When Agamemnon is murdered by his wife and her lover, Electra takes it upon her to avenge her father's death; in doing so she personifies the principle of revenge or, we may say, she acts as her father's spirit—or his ghost. When finally, with the help of her brother Orestes, Clytemnestra and Aegisthus are slain, does anybody regard this end as a triumph for Orestes? He, wielding the axe, is an instrument in his sister's hand, the tool of revenge. It is not even Electra who triumphs; it is in fact the principle of revenge (that primitive form of justice) that exults at being re-established once more, and Electra is merely the medium through which the emotion of triumphant justice finds its expression.

King Hamlet has no Electra who knows of the murder and might undertake to achieve retribution. So, bent on justice being done, he has to return from his tomb (as Agamemnon might have done had he not had his daughter); and the murdered husband walks and does not allow his cause to rest without trial. Yet when the trial is over and the question whether triumph or failure is to be answered, we have to consider the whole of the scheme and not only one single part in its execution, namely the part that has been allotted to Hamlet the son. Of this, Hamlet discharges himself not only honourably but even triumphantly as soon as his hands are free. What about the larger task, that which his father had set not to his son, but to himself?

Even if we restrict the answer to the detective story, which after all is the canvas of the picture, we can only congratulate old Hamlet on his most wonderful, indeed miraculous achievement. A ghost, an insubstantial spectre, succeeds in bringing to justice a ruling king for a crime for which no witness exists, of which no single soul has breathed the slightest hint of suspicion. For Claudius suddenly to find that after months of undisturbed security his deed has been discovered must be as incomprehensible as lightning out of the blue sky. But the disclosure of his crime is not all: the wrong is righted, the criminal punished. If that is not success, nothing is.

*

Yet there is more to King Hamlet's credit than the merely factual success of tracking down his own murderer; his is a real and great victory: the victory of forgiveness over revenge, of love over justice—the victory of the human heart.

In the days of Æschylus it would have been impossible to bring back to the stage the murdered Agamemnon and make him forgo his revenge and even forgive Clytemnestra. The Athenian audience, trained in older ideas of religion, morals, and justice, would have failed to understand that attitude. Two thousand years later—and it yields a little comfort, sorely needed indeed, to see that, measured by millennia, mankind is making progress after all—there now appears a man who had been deceived by his wife, with the result (to put it in a purposely vague manner) that he was murdered. He is not in the least unaware of what she had done; he speaks clearly of her adultery and does not minimize her guilt. Yet from the beginning he wishes to spare her any punishment or even recrimination: he forbids his son to contrive anything against her.

This son, young, inexperienced in the multifarious roughness of life, still full of the uncompromising idealism of youth, not yet acquainted with the bitter-sweet lesson that love can be as perilous as the passage between Scylla and Charybdis—this son insists on justice being meted out also (and even in the first place) to her who is his mother. He endeavours, as a preliminary, to find out the true extent of her guilt. But when he is just on the point of achieving his aim, his father intervenes. More than that:

159

the Ghost forgives the guilty woman, he does not cast a
stone at her, and he induces his son to forgive her also.
Nothing against Gertrude!—that is his main concern.
That assurance achieved, he returns to his tomb.

If he had to forgive her no more than her adultery he
acts in the most self-effacing manner; if he had to forgive
her more, then, one is almost tempted to say, he acts like
a Saint.

*

This play with the husband who returns from his tomb
and despite betrayal and murder protects his wife; with
the son who in obedience both to his father and his own
heart is prepared to quit this life in order to spare his
mother: this play is one of the great victories won for
mankind. Among the many Shakespeare has gained, this
is the greatest. It is the triumph of even-handed justice
and of all-forgiving love combined.

APPENDIX

Note A

"Hamlet" by Shakespeare, Dumas and Meurice

An Egyptian scholar, who himself had seen the production, told me that in the early 1930s at a Cairo theatre the play was given in a version in which not only Hamlet survives, having avenged the murder, but in which at the end the Ghost reappears. In a kind of apotheosis Hamlet literally ascends the throne; behind this a back-curtain opens and the Ghost with his own hands puts the crown on his son's head.

That, I thought, was the height of theatrical audacity. Since I was told, however, that the Arabic text had been a translation from the French, I did a little research work, of which this is the result.

On December 15th, 1847, at the *Théatre Historique* in Paris, the first performance took place of a *Hamlet* for the text of which Alexandre Dumas, the elder, and Paul Meurice were responsible. At the end of the last scene the Ghost appears in front of the whole Court and pronounces judgement. Addressing Laertes he says:

> Ton sang trop prompt t'entraîna vers l'abîme,
> Laërte, et le Seigneur t'a puni par ton crime.
> Mais tu le trouveras, car il sonde les coeurs,
> Moins sévère là-haut! Laërte,—prie et meurs!

Turning to the Queen he addresses her as follows:

> Ta faute était ton amour même,
> Ame trop faible, et Dieu vous aime quand on aime!
> Va, ton coeur a lavé sa honte avec ses pleurs:
> Femme ici, reine au ciel, Gertrude,—espère et meurs!

Towards Claudius, however, he is implacable:

> Pas de pardon! Va, meurtrier infâme!
> Pour tes crimes hideux, dans leur cercles de flamme,
> Les enfers dévorants n'ont pas trop de douleurs!
> Va, traître incestueux, va!—désespère et meurs!

Now Hamlet, still weary of life, asks what his own punishment is to be. His father pronounces: "Tu vivras!" —and on that the curtain comes down, thus cutting off all further controversy.

This so-called *Hamlet* had an uninterrupted run of 135 performances. Its version held the stage for twenty years. It was in this adaptation that in 1867 an actress, Mme. Judith, took the part of Hamlet, thus anticipating Sarah Bernhardt. She herself, however, had been antici- pated not only by a German actress, Felizitas Abt (about 1780), but by English actresses as well. The first of these was a Mrs. Furnivall in Dublin, 1741. She was followed by Sarah Siddons, who, about 1777, impersonated the Prince of Denmark in Manchester, Edinburgh, and Bristol, though never in London. A Mrs. Power took the part in 1797 at the Drury Lane, and a Mrs. Glover at the Lyceum Theatre in 1821.

*

Note B

THE TWO PICTURES

What are the two pictures: portraits hanging on the wall, or miniatures?

Edward Dowden, in *The Arden Shakespeare*, points out

that Restoration actors made Hamlet produce two miniatures; but miniatures, he adds, could hardly represent Hamlet's father at full length, as he is described. To this there is a twofold reply: first, that the miniature Hamlet describes as that of his father may in reality be a photograph of the actor's grandmother when she was a baby, and nobody in the audience would notice the fraud; and second, that a good many Elizabethan miniatures have come down to us that despite their size show full-length portraits.

Professor Dowden goes on to say:

A print, prefixed to Rowe's ed. of *Hamlet*, 1709, exhibits half-lengths hanging on the wall. The actor Holman had a picture of Claudius on the wall, and a miniature of the dead king produced from Hamlet's bosom. Fechter had two miniatures, one worn round Gertrude's neck, the other by Hamlet; he tore the miniature from Gertrude and flung it away; so Rossi, who stamped upon it. Edwin Booth used two miniatures. Sir H. Irving and Salvini have represented the portraits as seen only by the mind's eye.

Sir E. K. Chambers returns to the actor Holman's conception. "I have very little doubt," he says, "that Hamlet draws a miniature, a 'picture in little' (II. 2. 384), of his father from his pocket, and then turns to point at one of Claudius that hangs on the wall of the closet."

Professor Dover Wilson straightforwardly instructs the actor (not in a footnote or a commentary, but in a stage-direction proper): "Leads her to the portraits on the wall." In the Appendix he asserts that those two pictures are "full-length portraits". Can this conception be justified?

(1) In the nineteen lines in which he compares the two pictures Hamlet uses the word "this" eight times, the word "here" twice; not once does he say "that" or "there".

Look *here* upon *this* picture, and on *this* . . .
. . . seated on *this* brow . . .
This was your husband . . .
Here is your husband . . .
. . . *this* fair mountain . . .
. . . *this* moor . . .
. . . what judgement
Would step from *this* to *this*?

The continued use of "this" and "here" seems to indicate that the speaker has the pictures close at hand. Were he to draw Gertrude's attention to portraits on the wall, would he not, while pointing to at least one of them, say "that" picture, and "there"? Or are we, following Professor Wilson, to assume that both mother and son walk up to the paintings and stand in front of them? How impossible from the theatrical point of view! Moreover, is it probable that the Queen should have the pictures of both her husbands hang side by side, not in a state room, but in her closet? So shortly after her wedding? would there have been time for painting such a state portrait? Provided such a portrait was really available, would she not rather replace her first husband's picture by that of his successor? Furthermore, we know that Polonius hides himself behind the arras. (In Quarto 1 Corambis says expressly: "I'le shrowde my selfe behinde the Arras.") In a room, hung with tapestry, is it probable that there are full-length portraits on the wall, hung on the tapestry? And lastly, would it not be a great bother for the stage-manager to provide two large paintings that must show at least some likeness to the individual actors?

(2) In *Timon of Athens* the Painter is asked twice: "What have you there?" We cannot assume that it is a large canvas with a life-size portrait that he carries about. The Poet admires the "piece of painting" and says:

> . . . how this grace
> Speaks his own standing.

"Standing" may mean "station", i.e., "manner of standing," as in *Hamlet*, III. 4. 58:

> A station like the herald Mercury . . .

yet it may also mean the model's high rank. But then the Poet goes on to say:

> . . . to the dumbness of the gesture
> One might interpret.

The word "gesture" indicates that what the picture shows is not merely a head.

(3) In I. I. 160 Timon says:

> . . . These Pensil'd Figures are
> Euen such as they giue out.

The term "pencill'd" does not mean "painted" (see C. T. Onions, *A Shakespeare Glossary*). In his *Treatise concerning the Arte of Limning* (quoted by Mr. Carl Winter in *Elizabethan Miniatures*, The King Penguin Books, 1943) Nicholas Hillyarde, the famous "limner" of both Elizabeth and James, speaks of the art of "limning": he describes it as "a thing apart from all other painting or drawing", and says:

> Shadowing in lymning must not be driuen with the flat of the pensel as in oyle worke, distemper, or washing, but with the pointe of the pencell by lyttel light touches with cullor very thine. . . .

Thus the technical term "Pensil'd" turns out to be a proof that what Timon wishes to buy is a miniature.

(4) In the book just mentioned four miniatures are reproduced showing persons at full length. The smallest of them is slightly more than five by two inches.

In 1586, as we learn from Mr. Winter's Introduction, the Earl of Rutland paid £80 "for a brooch of her Majestie's picture in an agatt, set with fifty-three diamondes", and in 1603 a number of gentlemen "had cheynes given them by the King with his picture hanging".

(5) Was Shakespeare familiar with the custom among noblemen of wearing miniatures on chains round their necks? In *Twelfth Night* (III. 4. 231) we find:

Here, wear this jewel for me, 'tis my picture . . .

in *The Winter's Tale* (I. 2. 307):

He that wears her like her medal, hanging
About his neck . . .

and in *King Henry VIII* (II. 2. 31):

. . . a loss of her,
That like a jewel has hung twenty years
About his neck. . . .

Lastly, there is Hamlet himself who (in II. 2. 384) speaks of "pictures in little".

(6) There is one among Hillyarde's full-length miniatures that makes one almost believe that Shakespeare had seen it. It shows George Clifford, Earl of Cumberland, in the trappings of the Queen's Champion, with Gloriana's glove pinned to his hat. Hamlet's description of his father's portrait reads almost like a description of that miniature. The Earl stands on the top of a hill; there is a

166

wide outlook into the distance; three quarters of the background is sky. With outstretched arm he holds up a tilting-lance and his "station" as well as demeanour are challenging and proud. Here are indeed

> Hyperion's curls, the front of Jove himself,
> An eye like Mars, to threaten and command;
> A station like the herald Mercury
> New-lighted on a heaven-kissing hill.

—and all that on a miniature.

From the evidence produced there can, I think, be only one conclusion: that the two pictures Hamlet compares are miniatures.

*

Note C

ONE EXCEPTION

Separate from that chorus of consent is one solitary voice, that of Nicholas Rowe. He may rightly be called the father of Shakespeare criticism. After the four Folios, of which the latter three are on the whole mere reprints of the Folio 1623, he was the first to edit the plays: he divided the text into acts and scenes, added stage-directions, and so forth.

In an essay *Some Account of the Life, etc., of Mr. William Shakespear*, prefixed to his edition, published in 1709, he writes:

Hamlet is founded on much the same Tale with the *Electra* of *Sophocles*. In each of 'em a young Prince is engag'd to Revenge the Death of his Father, their Mothers are equally Guilty, are both concern'd in the Murder of their Husbands, and are afterwards married to the Murderers . . . *Hamlet* is represented with the same Piety towards his Father, and Resolution to Revenge his Death, as *Orestes*; he has the same Abhorrence for his Mother's Guilt, which, to provoke him the more, is heighten'd by Incest: But 'tis with wonderful Art and Justness of Judgment, that the Poet restrains him from doing Violence to his Mother. To prevent any thing of that Kind, he makes his Father's Ghost forbid that part of his Vengeance.

From this account it is evident that at the beginning of the eighteenth century, only three generations after the first performance of the play, the general conception was that Gertrude and Clytemnestra were "equally guilty"; Gertrude was "concern'd" in the murder of her husband. The idea that she might be innocent does not seem to have occurred to Rowe.

But, it may be said, Rowe was not a good editor: what evidence is there that his opinion is of any weight? Against this several points have to be considered.

Rowe was not a hack writer; he was poet laureate. He wrote many plays, some of which were staged at the Haymarket and Drury Lane Theatres. In two of his tragedies the leading parts were, in later years, taken by Sarah Siddons. His insight into theatrical matters cannot have been dim.

He was, moreover, a friend of Betterton's. It was Betterton who told him that Shakespeare's impersonation of the Ghost in *Hamlet* was "the top of his performance". Betterton on his part was as early as 1661 a member of Sir William D'Avenant's theatrical company. Sir William was Shakespeare's godson (or, as rumour had it, his natural son). Thus a direct line leads from D'Avenant through Betterton to Rowe, and it is not impossible that traditional elements, at least as to the general conception of the play, were still preserved and handed down.

Betterton, who died in 1710, eight years before Rowe, was not only highly esteemed as an actor, but was also a playwright; he should have been well fitted to discern a vital point such as the question of Gertrude's guilt or innocence.

Considering all the circumstances it seems reasonably certain to assume that in the performances in which Betterton was Hamlet, the Queen played her part in such a way that she appeared as an accomplice in the murder; or it would have been hardly possible for Rowe to write, as he did, of Gertrude's being "concern'd" in the murder. Rowe was a great admirer of Betterton's Hamlet and must have seen his performance more than once. His testimony should not be cast to the winds.

*

Note D

"... ARTLESS JEALOUSY ..."

The expression "artless jealousy" has been paraphrased by "irrepressible misgiving". Can this be justified?

In C. T. Onions, *A Shakespeare Glossary*, a somewhat different explanation, identical with that of the *Clarendon Edition*, 1872, is given, namely: "Guilt is so full of suspicion that it unskilfully betrays itself in fearing to be betrayed."

As to "jealousy" we find:

(1) in *Julius Cæsar*, I. 2. 71, Cassius says to Brutus:

And be not jealous on me, gentle Brutus:

The question of "jealousy" in the modern sense of the word does not come in here; Cassius merely asks his friend not to *distrust* him.

(2) *Julius Cæsar*, I. 2. 161:

That you do love me I am nothing jealous.

Brutus speaks to Cassius. Again there is no question of "jealousy"; he merely says that as to the other's friendship he has no *doubt* or *suspicion*.

(3) *Venus and Adonis*, 321:

When lo! the unback'd breeder, full of fear,
Jealous of catching, swiftly doth forsake him. . . .

"Jealous of catching" means "*afraid* of being caught".

(4) *Hamlet*, II. I. 113: Polonius, on learning of the Prince's "madness", exclaims:

I fear'd he did but trifle
And meant to wrack thee; but beshrew my jealousy.

He curses his *mistrustfulness*.

(5) *King Henry V*, IV. I. 305:

My lord, your nobles, jealous of your absence,
Seek through your camp to find you.

They look for the King because they have the *misgiving* lest he might be absent.

(7) *Twelfth-Night*, III. 3. 8:

> . . . jealousy what might befall your travel. . . .

Antonio speaks of his *anxiety* or *misgiving* lest something might befall his friend on his journey.

Turning now to "artless", we should, first, keep in mind that in Shakespeare "art", as far as it is an equivalent to "skill", often savours of "cunning". This shade of meaning has survived in "artful", as far as "artfulness" means "deceitfulness" or "wiliness". (In his Preface to Shakespeare, Vol VIII, p. 472, Dr. Johnson, 1765, describes Othello as "magnanimous, artless, and credulous", where "artless" apparently means "lacking in the art of dissimulation".)

Secondly, "artless" does in our passage not mean "lacking in art", but denotes a case in which art is "of no avail". In *King Lear*, IV. 6. 39, Gloucester, addressing the "mighty gods", speaks of their "opposeless wills", i.e., where opposition is of no avail. In *Venus and Adonis*, 604, birds are spoken of, "deceiv'd with painted grapes":

> As those poor birds that helpless berries saw.

In *A Lover's Complaint*:

> . . . that phraseless hand. . . .

—which no phrase can describe. In Spenser's *An Hymne in Honour of Love* we find:

> resistless hand. . . .

—i.e., a hand "to resist which is of no avail". In *Paradise Regained*, IV. 268:

> resistless eloquence. . . .

—meaning "that cannot be resisted". In *The Jew of Malta*, III:

> . . . the wasteful sea,
> Whose billows, beating the resistless banks. . . .

—and Dr. Samuel Johnson uses the phrase "resistless authority".

In conclusion, therefore, "artless jealousy" seems to mean perturbation which to allay art (the art of dissimulation) is of no avail; or: fearfulness which no art(fulness) can subdue; or, paraphrased: "irrepressible misgiving".

*

Note E

QUOTATIONS

William Hazlitt, dealing with Hamlet (in his *Characters of Shakespear's Plays*, 1817), quotes the passage: "Now might I do it pat. . . ." In his version, however, the line:

> O, this is hire and salary, not revenge

reads differently, namely:

> Why, this is reward, not revenge.

The words: "now he is praying" have become: "He kneels and prays"; and the lines:

> A villain kills my father, and for that,
> I, his sole son, do this same villain send
> To heaven. . . .

have been paraphrased like this:

172

He kill'd my father, and for that,
I, his sole son, send him to heaven.

And then Hazlitt goes on to say: "He is the prince of philosophical speculators." Yet is not Hazlitt's view on Hamlet's speculations somewhat warped if he does not know what the prince of speculators really says?

If we look for other quotations: Hazlitt's Ophelia was not "sewing" in her closet, but "reading"; Hamlet's stockings were not "foul'd" but "loose"; there is no "willow grows aslant a brook", but a "willow hanging o'er a brook", and so forth.

These deviations are not due to bad memory; Hazlitt does not quote the passages by heart (as Charles Lamb occasionally does with similar results). He quotes correctly, but from some Player Quarto. It is strange that so great a critic should have cared so little for the "True Originall Copies", and one wonders whether in assessing Shakespeare's genius Hazlitt was not hampered to some extent, at least as far as the poet's language is concerned, by his blind reliance on what those unscrupulous Restoration players had done to the text.

Even Dr. Bradley's quotations are sometimes inaccurate. When dealing, e.g., with Hamlet's hesitation to kill the King who kneels and attempts to pray, he quotes:

. . . and so he goes to heaven:
And so I am revenged. That would be scanned.

—and he continues: "He scans it; and the sword . . . is thrust back into its sheath." He puts a full stop after "scanned". Quarto 2, however, has no stop there at all, and the Folio has a clear comma:

And so I am reueng'd: that would be scann'd,
A Villaine killes my Father, and for that. . . .

173

Bradley, by putting or accepting that full stop, makes Hamlet say: "That demands to be considered (by me)"; and then he goes on to consider it: "A villain kills my father, and for that . . ." But if pointed as in the Folio: "That would be scann'd, a villain . . .", the meaning is: "If I did it, that would be considered (by the others) that a villain has killed my father, and for that . . ." Bradley makes Hamlet struggle with himself whether to do it or not; but the Folio shows him here as imagining what his country would think of the deed if done. A difference of no small import.

To my mind we have here yet another indication of Hamlet's desire to differentiate between murder and judgement: he wishes to proceed not as an assassin but as a judge. Here again he is very seriously concerned about his own reputation; he does not wish that "a wounded name" should live behind him.

*

Note F

"HOW ALL OCCASIONS . . ."

There can be no doubt that this soliloquy has been penned by Shakespeare himself.

(a)

First, we find in it all the happy irregularities in scansion and versification that, in the maturity of his style, are so characteristic of Shakespeare's diction and ways of declamation. In particular there are several instances of two or even three stresses clashing, a peculiarity that must be regarded as one of the true hall-marks of his dramatic diction.

A thought which, quarter'd, hath but one part wisdom
x — x — x / x x — — — x
Witness this army of such mass and charge
— x x — x x — — x —
When honour's at the stake. How stand I then
x — x x x — / (x) / — x — x
To hide the slain? O, from this time forth
x — x — / (x) / — x — x —
My thoughts be bloody, or be nothing worth.
x — — — x / x x — x —

(b)

Then there is the fact that the monologue is yet another friendly clash with Montaigne, with whom in those years, and especially when writing his *Hamlet*, Shakespeare so often crossed swords. It is not so much that he "borrows" from Montaigne, but that he replies to him. It is a kind of discussion between kindred souls. How Montaigne would have loved to read the open or underhand answers —if only he had lived a dozen years longer! The great mind would have made a deep bow to the greater heart.

Whether Shakespeare read Montaigne's *Essays* in the original or in John Florio's translation we do not know. Florio's text was published only in 1603, but he had the book entered in the Stationers' Register on June 4th, 1600, and it is not improbable that Shakespeare had access to the manuscript through his patron, the Earl of Southampton, in whose "pay and patronage" Florio himself says he had lived for several years.

One of Florio's personal friends was Ben Jonson, who in a presentation copy of his *Volpone*, 1607, wrote the dedication: "To his Louing Father and worthy Freind

Mr. John Florio, the ayde of his Muses, Ben: Jonson seales this testemony of Freindship and Loue." In the same *Volpone*, in III. 2, Ben Jonson makes Lady Politick Would-be say:

> All our English writers,
> I mean such as are happy in the Italian,
> Will deign to steal out of this author, mainly:
> Almost as much as from Montagnié.

In the twelfth chapter of his second book Montaigne speaks of the reasons for going to war:

> Quant à la guerre, qui est la plus grande et pompeuse des actions humaines, je sçaurois volontiers si nous nous en voulons servir pour argument de quelque prerogative, ou, au rebours, pour tesmoignage de nostre imbecillité et imperfection; comme de vray, la science de nous entredesfaire et entretuer, de ruyner et perdre nostre propre espece, il semble qu'elle n'a beaucoup de quoy se faire desirer aux bestes qui ne l'ont pas. . . .
> . . . cette effroyable ordonnance de tant de milliers d'hommes armez, tant de fureur, d'ardeur et de courage, il est plaisant à considerer par combien vaines occasions elle est agitee, et par combien legieres occasions esteincte.

It seems as if it were to this example of Montaigne's sceptical wordly-mindedness that the youthfully enthusiastic Hamlet replies: Yes, that may all happen; many thousands may be led to their graves. But what does it matter,

> When honour's at the stake?

(c)

There can be no question that "How all occasions" is a

176

genuine brother of "To be or not to be"; an older brother and in the end displaced and got rid of, but still a brother who, had not the younger come into being, would have proved most royally. And yet, two brothers are never alike, even if twins, and between the two soliloquies there is a great difference.

The Hamlet of "How all occasions" is not yet where the other Hamlet has arrived when he ponders over "To be or not to be"; he is still hesitating; he cannot prevail on himself to do the deed of revenge. Why? For one reason: he is still too much bound to this earthly life.

He searches his own heart: why has he not yet killed his uncle? Is it bestial oblivion? Certainly not. Then it is

> some craven scruple
> Of thinking too precisely on the event,
> A thought which, quarter'd, hath but one part wisdom
> And ever three parts coward. . . .

What is this event? "Event", used here in its literal sense, means "outcome". The outcome of what? As Hamlet himself says, the thought of it is three-quarters cowardice. What he is thinking of is his own death. He apparently assumes that to kill Claudius might cost him, Hamlet, his own life. By this trend of thought he shows that he, this Hamlet, has not yet decided to proceed against the King in full daylight, acting as a judge, but is still occupied by the cruder idea that he would have to slay him at the first chance offered, even at the risk of being, as a regicide, slain himself by the loyal Danes.

This Hamlet is not identical with our Hamlet. He obviously belongs to an earlier plan, later supplanted by the play as we have it.

This understudy differs from the real Hamlet in one vital point, in that of death: as to dying he needs self-persuasion. Look at that delicate and tender prince, he says to himself; he "makes mouths at the invisible event", i.e., he scorns the unforeseen outcome: he indeed is prepared to sacrifice all, even his life,

> When honour's at the stake.—How stand I then . . .

and so forth. He—another Claudio (*Measure for Measure*) —shrinks back from the image of death. The idea of dying is an obstacle in his path, a stone that must be removed: that is the purpose of his soliloquy. His brother is far in advance of him, in resolution as well as philosophy; he has already shaken himself free from these earthly fetters. What he is concerned about is not dying, but what comes thereafter—when we have shuffled off this mortal coil, what dreams may come.

"Two stars keep not their motion in one sphere", and if we find two Hamlets in the play, the one struggling to overcome his fear of death, the other so little concerned with death that already he stands beyond the border, as it were, looking back on his life, then there can be no doubt that one of the two is out of place. A chrysalis develops into a butterfly, but the butterfly cannot creep back into the cocoon which in freeing itself it has broken.

(d)

There is, finally, yet another consideration. In *Der Bestrafte Brudermord*, II. 5, Hamlet says:

> My dear friend Horatio, with the help of this simulated madness I hope to find an opportunity to avenge the murder of my father. But as you know, my father is always surrounded by many guards; therefore, should I fail and you perchance find my corpse, give it a decent burial, for on the first occasion I find I shall make an attempt on him.

178

A second time, in II. 9, after the play-scene, that German Hamlet tells Horatio:

From this hour onward I shall try my best, wherever I find the King by himself, to take his life.

It is highly probable that *Der Bestrafte Brudermord* goes back to, or shows traces of, some Ur-Hamlet, either Kyd's play or Shakespeare's own first draft. If so, the passages quoted make it clear that that predecessor of Hamlet intends to kill his uncle as soon as opportunity offers, even at the risk of sacrificing his own life: ". . . should I fail and you perchance find my corpse. . . ."

I submit that the soliloquy: "How all occasions," where we have the thinking "on the event, A thought which . . . hath . . . three parts coward", may well come from the lips of that Ur-Hamlet, who is bent on brute assassination, but cannot come from the Hamlet of the final play, who wishes to proceed as a judge. It is not "hire and salary" that our Hamlet seeks, but "revenge".*

*

Note G

"WHAT POOR AN INSTRUMENT . . ."

It is rather astonishing to see that Dr. Bradley, comparing the Porter in *Macbeth* with "the old Countryman who brings the asps to Cleopatra", speaks of "our untroubled amusement" at the latter and thinks "it was right to make him really comic". Was ever producer so misguided as to make that "rural fellow" perform his part in a "really comic" way?

* It is perhaps not without significance that Thomas Betterton never spoke the soliloquy: "How all occasions . . . ".

Cleopatra has prepared for that exigency. She sends Charmian forth and says:

I have spoke already, and it is provided.

When Charmian returns, the Queen adorns herself for her death; and when the "rural fellow" is announced she exclaims, even before he enters:

What poor an instrument
May do a noble deed: he brings me liberty.

The man on the other hand knows well enough for what purpose he delivers the serpents, hidden in his basket beneath a layer of figs. He brings her liberty, as she calls it; but, to him, what he offers her with trembling hands is death. He hides his horror beneath a layer of fun—and the result of that mixture is a danse macabre in words.

The thought veers back to another "poor instrument"——

Come hither, man: I see that thou art poor . . .

—to the Apothecary in *Romeo and Juliet*. Shakespeare made him a half-starved beggar, but he did not make him comic. To the young poet death was still something that evokes awe. Only in his later plays does it happen that death is greeted with bells joyfully tinkling on his fools' caps. Lear's Fool "goes to bed at noon". In *Measure for Measure*, Pompey and Abhorson, appointed to execute Claudio, poke the crudest fun at their "mystery", and the Clown in *Hamlet* "sings at grave-making". O death, where is thy sting?

Why, I ask myself, was I so astonished to see that

Dr. Bradley takes that "Countryman" as merely comic? It is probably due to a very early impression on my memory. With *Antony and Cleopatra* (if I may insert a personal reminiscence) it was as with so many other Shakespeare plays: I had seen practically all of them on the stage before I had read them. The first production of *Antony and Cleopatra* I ever saw goes back more than thirty years and I have only a dim recollection of it; of the protagonists I can scarcely remember anything at all. And yet, I still see before me that "rural fellow", baring his teeth in a broad grin that was truly frightening. The words he spoke were funny; yet it was plain that with all his jokes he only endeavoured to conceal the fearfulness of his duty. He tried to make the Queen laugh, but he only revealed his heart that was full of pity. He was a human being, a very odd one at that; yet there was an aura around him that made him appear ghostlike—a messenger from the world beyond.

At the Burgtheater in Vienna no role in a Shakespeare play was considered as of second-rate importance. The actor who took the part of that Clown (his name was Heine) played on other occasions the parts of Julius Cæsar and Iago.

*

Note H

THEME AND VARIATIONS

Was I sufficiently cautious in expressing my view on how Hamlet faces his end? I have suggested that he enters the "fencing-match" with open eyes, fully aware that in all likelihood he is going to meet his death; he "embraces freely" what is "to come"—"the readiness is all".

I was not always so cautious. In 1936, after I had translated the play, I published a small book on it. ("Hamlets Flucht in den Tod," Herbert Reichner Verlag, Vienna.) In this I put forward and expounded the opinion that Hamlet deliberately walks into the Mouse-trap, now set for him, and that so to speak he uses Laertes as a means to commit suicide.

That suggestion, I feel sure now, went too far. And although since that attempt to solve the mystery of Hamlet's psychology a dozen years have gone by I confess to being very glad indeed that this present inquiry is primarily concerned with the Ghost and not with his son; perhaps in another twelve years I may feel better equipped to write on Hamlet himself. Still, what at that time induced me to assume that Hamlet actually seeks to quit this world is perhaps interesting enough to be summarized in a few paragraphs.

Shakespeare's mind works like a prism of crystal: it has no colour itself, but it has the faculty of dividing a ray of light into its component colours. (It has another quality too: whatever passes through it, the prism itself remains cool, impartial, unmoved. That is why so little is known about Shakespeare's own personality.)

As soon as a dramatic idea enters his mind Shakespeare instantly divides it into its component parts, complementary or correlative. By that process, it seems, he endows his characters with something that might be called three-dimensionality.

It would not be enough to say that by creating a figure of contrast he provides his main character with a shadow, and thus with corporality. Shadows can be painted; and in fact if we look at a conversation piece of Hogarth's we find a great number of shadows. Still, his pictures are two-dimensional only, and so are plays by Ben Jonson or Molière, even if put on the stage. Shakespeare's characters need more, and have more: they have a third dimension. They step forth from the canvas and show themselves to be figures just as we are, figures round whom we can walk. (They show less reality than we do, but greater truth.) This effect is achieved by that magic squint in Shakespeare's mind that enables—or coerces—him to see one idea from two or three angles simultaneously. (He himself speaks of

> The poet's eye, in a fine frenzy rolling,

that "turns to shapes . . . the forms of things unknown" —which after all is only a poetic expression for that mental strabism.)

In *A Midsummer-Night's Dream* the central idea—that single ray of light—is the polarity of love and hatred. Hermia loves Lysander and hates Demetrius. Demetrius, scorned by Hermia, scorns Helena, who follows him in vain. Handy-dandy, change places! Titania falls out with Oberon, but falls in love with the ass for whom, after the night, she feels nothing but loathing. Even Hippolyta and Theseus are a changed couple; first they were enemies, at war with each other:

> Hippolyta, I woo'd thee with my sword,
> And won thy love doing thee injury.

The theme of *Twelfth Night* is unrequited love, followed up through half a dozen variations. Orsino loves Olivia—in vain; Olivia loves Cesario—hopelessly; Viola loves Orsino—her love is a "blank"; Sir Andrew loves Olivia—to very little purpose; Antonio follows Sebastian, only to see him married to Olivia; and even Malvolio persuades himself he has fallen in love with his mistress—to all of whom has to be added that imaginary sister of Cesario who "never told her love, but . . . sat like Patience on a monument".

In *King Lear* we have first the relation between Lear and his daughters paralleled by Gloucester and his sons. Another motif is that of "madness": Lear's madness is contrasted with Edgar's assumed madness and with the Fool's maddened and maddening jokes. There is scarcely a single play that would not provide us with similar instances of theme and variations.

In *Hamlet*, too, there are parallels over parallels. Hamlet's father is dead. So is the older Fortinbras: he was slain by King Hamlet. Hamlet is deprived of the succession to the throne; his uncle is King of Denmark. Fortinbras is in a similar position: his uncle, though bed-ridden, is King of Norway. Hamlet has been given the task of avenging his father's death; Laertes, whose father too has been killed (making the third father) regards revenge as his given duty.

How these two acquit themselves of their responsibilities is clearly shown. Yet is not Fortinbras, too, intent on revenge? And does he not, though belatedly, achieve it? Before the action proper begins, we learn about King Hamlet that "our valiant Hamlet" slew King Fortinbras and took part of his land. Still in the same first act we hear repeatedly that young Fortinbras demands the return of "those foresaid lands So by his father lost", that he insists on "the surrender of those lands lost by his father", and the very last development in the play is that the son of King Fortinbras, slain by Hamlet's father, takes over those lands. "Blood will have blood"; the end is connected with the beginning, and thus the whole play is put as it were in a frame. Three sons have avenged their fathers; only one survives: he with whose father's blood the story had begun.

Nor do the parallels end there. We have Hamlet's feigned madness contrasted with Ophelia's genuine

184

insanity. We have the picture (the old trick practised by artists: a picture within a picture) showing Pyrrhus with his sword raised, but stopping it in mid-air, just as later Hamlet, himself stands behind Claudius, his sword in hand, but not using it. And finally we have the suicide motif.

Ophelia drowns herself. Horatio wishes to be "an antique Roman" and would take his own life but for Hamlet, who, dying himself, wrenches the poisoned cup from his hand. Seeing these two variations I put the question whether we are not justified in assuming that the theme itself cannot be far away, and whether Hamlet does not more than merely speak of suicide.

I was misguided by the assumption that the main motif of the play is to be found in the question of suicide. As I see it now, the real theme of *Hamlet* is something different: it is the polarity of revenge and forgiveness, the conflict between justice and mercy—a conflict fought out in two hearts, the one being that of the husband, the other that of the son.

*

Note I

Goethe's Conception of Hamlet

It is Goethe with whom those scruples started. Yet if we wish to understand how he came by his somewhat peculiar view of Hamlet's appearance as well as mind we have to go back to Wieland; for it is through Wieland's eyes and in his translation that Goethe made the acquaintance of Hamlet.

In his text of the play, published in 1767, Wieland omitted the first part of v. 2 altogether, i.e., the dialogue in which Hamlet tells Horatio of his voyage to England. Instead, Wieland gives in his own words a short summary of its contents. And there, in a lengthy footnote, referring to Hamlet's wish to be reconciled with Laertes, Wieland puts forth his own conception of the hero's character:

From this, one can deduce that Hamlet has designs upon the King; but it is nothing definite, no real scheme. He has been given the task to avenge his father's death; he wishes to fulfil that task, and yet, from the outset to the very end he never knows how to set about it or how to put it into practice. . . . Throughout the play he is swayed less by passion than moodiness. His melancholy is cold, ruminative, eccentric. Only now and then are there sudden gusts of passion, as quickly subsiding as they have broken forth. He is indifferent as to his own life; the great task of revenge, with which his soul is swelling, he leaves to mere chance; and he does not think it worth while to work out a plan or to take precautions lest he himself be involved in his enemy's fall.

It is evident that this view greatly influenced Goethe's conception of Hamlet. It is always the first impression that strikes the deepest root. Nor did Wieland's influence consist only in what he said on Hamlet, but also in the manner he translated the play.

Wieland stood with both feet in that literature of youthful romanticism to which Goethe himself was so outstanding a contributor. It was the time of unashamed sentimentality, when remembrance-books were filled with protestations, more or less well-rhymed, of never-dying emotions, when locks cut from the beloved's head were worn in medallions round the neck, and when young men

186

shed tears on altars of friendship, erected in shaded forest glades. It was the time of *Werther*. This emotional trend towards delicacy and tender-heartedness rather than passion and vigour fashioned to some extent Wieland's language by sentimentalizing it. Little wonder, therefore, that Goethe, when Hamlet was presented to him in that garb of pale shades, thought he had found a kindred soul, almost a cousin of his own Werther.

Nor is that all; Wieland's text contains a number of downright mistranslations that still more obscured the strangely dim light in which Goethe saw the Prince of Denmark. Gertrude's words in the last scene:

He's fat, and scant of breath

mean of course that Hamlet is perspiring and that the fight, having gone on for some time, has made him gasp for breath. Wieland, however, translated:

Er ist zu fett und von zu kurzem Athem

—i.e., "he is too stout and too short-winded," making Hamlet constitutionally asthmatic as well as corpulent. Accordingly (in v. 6 of *Wilhelm Meister*) Goethe speaks of Hamlet as being "flabby" and describes him thus:

In the fencing-match he is hard put to it; sweat is running down his face, and the Queen says: He is stout, let him regain his breath. . . . Is not also his vacillating melancholy, his languid grief, his lack of active decision more in accordance with such a figure than a slim youth with auburn locks, of whom one would expect more initiative and dexterity?*

* Prof. Allardyce Nicoll takes "fat" to mean "stout". He sees Hamlet as "a robust soldier, accustomed to manly exercise, but a trifle out of form owing to his sojourn at the Danish Court, and hence stout. . . ."

Another mistranslation had still more serious consequences. At the end of Act I Hamlet exclaims:

The time is out of joint: O curséd spite,
That ever I was born to set it right!

This was rendered by Wieland as follows:

Die Zeit ist aus ihren Fugen gekommen; o! unseliger Zufall! dass ich gebohren werden musste, sie wieder zurecht zu sezen!

—which, retranslated, means:

The time has got out of joint; oh, unhappy chance that I should have been born to set it right again!

The "curséd spite" has been whittled down to "unhappy chance": what in the original is a challenge has become a complaint.

To realize the influence this particular mistranslation had on Goethe we need only look up how he describes his asthmatic hero at the end of Act I, when his father's ghost has left him to himself. There Goethe says:

Amazement and melancholy overcome the solitary figure. . . . He swears never to forget the departed spirit and concludes with the expressive sigh: "The time is out of joint; woe is me that I was born to set it right!"

He goes even one step further than Wieland: instead of "oh, unhappy chance" he lets Hamlet exclaim—no, "conclude with a sigh": "woe is me!" Shakespeare's Hamlet curses his fate; Goethe's Hamlet heaves a sigh. The one defies his lot, the other yields to it. There, in a nut-shell, we have the difference between the two conceptions.

And then Goethe goes on to say:

> In these words, methinks, lies the key to Hamlet's whole character . . . a great deed laid upon a soul that is not equal to it.

It is a straight and direct line that leads from mistranslation to misinterpretation. For Goethe, Hamlet was a sentimentalist, lacking in inner and outer strength, an avenger balked and thwarted not by circumstances, but by his own weakness. Shakespeare's Hamlet speaks of suicide, but it is a great query whether he would ever commit it. Had it fallen to Goethe to write the play, his Hamlet would have blown out his brains—as his Werther did.

The whole thing is another Leaning Tower of Pisa. At the base there lies a small mistranslation, its bias seemingly negligible. Yet the edifice built on that mistake must necessarily become lopsided, the more so the higher the psychological regions to which it is raised.

The confusion was aggravated by the fact that the English-speaking scholars who expounded Goethe's conception, either accepting or repudiating it, were under the impression that both sides were talking of one and the same subject. That, however, was not the case; Goethe saw and criticized a different Hamlet, one not only clad in foreign language, but one whose mental and psychological make-up had considerably changed. Thus it is that in those controversies, as soon as the argument turns to Goethe's judgement, as it inevitably does, the disputants find themselves promptly at cross purposes, the reason being that they talk of different persons. One might quote Hamlet himself: "Look here upon this picture, and on this," of which the second is certainly a "counterfeit presentment".

The divergence between the two Hamlet conceptions

has of course been noticed, but not the divergence between the two Hamlets. The explanation is simple; it lies in the fact that most scholars when reading *Wilhelm Meister* make use of Carlyle's translation.* In this, the sage of Cheyne Row occasionally takes liberties with the text, rendering sometimes not what Goethe has written but what, in the translator's opinion, he ought to have written. In the passage, e.g., quoted above he renders Goethe's words: "bedeutender Seufzer" not with "expressive sigh" as I have done, but with "significant ejaculation", an expression that modifies the psychological import of the passage.

Another point is that Carlyle did not bother to retranslate verbally into English the passages from *Hamlet* as he found them—with their mistakes—in the German text. Without thinking of any possible harm he simply had recourse to the original, inserting the quotations in Shakespeare's own words. By doing so he unwittingly concealed the fact that Goethe, when dealing with Hamlet's character, had someone in mind who so to speak was a younger brother only of the real Hamlet. Hence all the disparity and discord.

*

Note J

GOETHE AS PRODUCER OF "HAMLET"

What Goethe, the poet, thought of the play and also how it should be produced is not difficult to find out: one

* Prof. Dover Wilson, Sir E. K. Chambers, Mr. Waldock, etc.

has only to read the chapters in *Wilhelm Meisters Lehrjahre* that deal with the matter. It is, however, less easy to discover what Goethe, the theatrical producer, did when he staged the play at the Weimar Theatre, of which he was managing director for twenty-two years.

Up to 1791 the citizens of Weimar had to rely on travelling companies. One of them, the *Bellomo Troupe*, had *Hamlet* on their repertoire, and when visiting the town used to perform the play. They gave it in a prose version in which there was no Laertes and no Fortinbras either. The Graveyard-scene was omitted altogether and there was no fencing-match at the end. Hamlet takes his revenge after all and ascends the throne. The responsibility for this adaptation lies with F. L. Schröder, the director of the Hamburg theatre.

As early as 1792, however, Goethe staged *Hamlet* himself, this time with the personnel of his own theatre. In the playbill the audience was assured that the play was to be given "Entirely according to the original". The term "entirely" was not entirely true. Once more Schroeder's version was made use of, once more there was no Fortinbras, and so we cannot but assume that Goethe, too, was reluctant to dispatch Hamlet into "the undiscover'd country". Again there was no Laertes, and Horatio, too, had disappeared from the dramatis personæ. The bold announcement: "Entirely true to the original" only shows that the world of the stage has at all times been a world of (more or less pious) fraud, even with a Goethe as its presiding genius.

That age of Enlightenment was very much in favour of justice being done; but they disagreed with the idea that the judge should share the fate of the culprits. For them, a tragedy ought to be a morality also. Events, however cruel and sad, should end in the final triumph of the good and righteous, in an end such as Nahum Tate had provided for his version of *King Lear*: it culminates in

those rainbow verses that would have been the true motto
for every tragedy of those days:

> Thy bright Example shall convince the World
> (Whatever Storms of Fortune are decreed)
> That Truth and Vertue shall at last succeed.

The popular cry wanted Hamlet to survive—and Goethe
gave in. We wonder at that all the more as Goethe, just in
connection with *Hamlet*, has written these golden words:
"It is base submission to the multitude to stir in them the
emotions they *wish* to have, instead of those they *ought*
to have."

In later years one of the actors at the Weimar Theatre
was P. A. Wolff, engaged there from 1803–16. Goethe
repeatedly spoke and wrote of him as his favourite
disciple. When in 1809 Wolff was to play the part of
Hamlet (this time in Schlegel's translation) Goethe
coached him for many weeks carefully. Every attitude
and motion, we are told, was discussed and everything
rejected that was regarded as contrary to the "Rules for
Actors", which Goethe had noted down. One of these
Rules reads as follows: "When changing gestures or
postures it is to be kept in mind that such changes must
be appropriately prepared and executed slowly, and in no
case during a speech."

Having left Weimar, Wolff toured the German theatres,
and in 1818 played Hamlet at Leipzig. In a local paper,
the *Morgenblatt für gebildete Stände*, there appeared a
criticism of his performance in which we read:

> The exchange of rapiers was most ingeniously arranged
> for by the insertion of a few explanatory words. When
> Hamlet feels he is wounded, he complains about
> Laertes's dishonesty in making use, in a mere sword-
> play, of a pointed weapon. While demanding satis-

192

faction he throws his own rapier down, wrenches the pointed one from his opponent's hand, and thus makes the poet's intention clearly visible.

Trying to find out who had the audacity to invent and insert those "few explanatory words" we arrive at the astonishing fact that it was Goethe himself. In his own hand the lines have not been preserved. In 1825 the theatre at Weimar went up in flames and in the fire the stage-book of *Hamlet* was destroyed. Yet shortly afterwards a new stage-book was prepared, and there we find the following lines which, all circumstances considered, must be regarded as Goethe's own addition to Shakespeare's text.

When Hamlet receives the wound he exclaims:

Ha, what is this, Laertes? I am wounded!
What, do you call it honesty and friendship,
While we are playing for the sake of practice,
To use a rapier with the point unbated?
Give satisfaction, let's exchange the weapons!

As a poet, how often is Goethe the father of obscurity! As a stage-producer, however, he was all for transparent lucidity; everything should be clearly motivated, easily intelligible and plainly visible. True, those inserted lines make the exchange of rapiers both reasonable and easy to perform; yet the question remains whether it is permissible for any stage-producer to meddle with the text. Since Shakespeare did not write those "few explanatory words" himself, but wishes the two antagonists to exchange their weapons without exchanging words, he must have good reasons for it. It is for us to find out these reasons and to make the stage proceedings conform to them.

*

Note K

THE EXCHANGE OF RAPIERS

How indeed do they come by one another's weapon? Many suggestions have been proffered. Yet since the whole duel, including the last and decisive bout, is fought in almost complete silence we cannot possibly say, this conception is right and that is wrong.

Professor Dover Wilson, accepting a suggestion put forward by Mr. Evan John, describes the action like this: Hamlet, he says,

> suddenly dropping to the ground the foil in his right, seizes with the empty hand the hilt of the sword he covets and wrests it from his enemy's grasp. The feat, we may be sure, is greeted with thunders of applause from the spectators in the theatre, as he pauses in ironical courtesy to allow Laertes to pick up the discarded foil . . . this was, in general, I believe, the way the fatal match was played out on the Globe stage in 1601.

It may have been so; we have no means of knowing. It seems to me, however, that this interpretation makes Hamlet's behaviour highly undignified. Would he really, after such a vulgar shindy, resume the fencing with its elaborate rules and regulations? Why not at once take his enemy by the throat and strangle him?

Without venturing to suggest that my idea is the correct one, I propose to describe the fight as it was played in that Vienna production, already referred to, in which my translation was made use of. (The match was fought with rapiers only, omitting the daggers.)

Laertes, enraged at his failure so far to achieve a hit,

194

drops at last the pretence of a mere play: at "Have at you now!", disregarding the rules of fencing, and knowing his opponent's weapon to be abated and therefore harmless, he brutally breaks through Hamlet's defence and lands his thrust. At once he jumps back to save himself from his victim's wrath. There he stands, half turned aside, clearly showing his guilty conscience, but at the same time apprehensively watching his enemy: how will he react?

Hamlet has stepped back. With his left hand he feels his wound—a wound in his chest—and looks at his fingers as though they showed blood. A knowing smile plays round his lips. Slowly, very slowly, thus increasing the threat of his procedure, he crosses the stage towards Laertes, who, before that menacing stare, shrinks further back, holding his rapier ready to protect himself. Coming within reach, Hamlet with one single blow strikes at Laertes's sword. It drops to the ground. Laertes, without taking his eyes from his enemy, tries to bend his knee in an attempt to regain his weapon; but Hamlet, with a majestic and irresistible gesture, forces his own sword into Laertes's hand. Then, knowing that now no real danger can come from his opponent's hand, he picks up the unbated rapier—and they continue the fight. The King, in an endeavour to rescue his minion's life, tries to stop the match ("Part them, they are incensed"); but Hamlet ("Nay, come again") attacks and takes his revenge.

In this arrangement the exchange of rapiers is not left to physical violence, displayed in an ugly brawl, but to psychological means: on the one side bad conscience and cowardice, on the other the commanding grandeur of a truly great mind, enhanced by the dignity of a prince who is the victim of foul treachery.

I watched the scene more than once: each time the audience followed the action in breathless silence.

*

Note L

THE STAGING OF THE PLAY

In the following I venture to give an account of how I think the play was produced at the Globe Theatre.

We have to visualize the two stages, the upper stage (the balcony or gallery) and the lower stage with its protruding "apron". We have further to keep in mind that the words "stage" and "enter", as used in Quartos and Folio, may refer to either stage, both of which combined constitute "the stage".

In the stage-directions the balcony is sometimes referred to as "aloft" or "above" or "a window", etc. In the texts, however, the upper stage is usually merely hinted at, or if mentioned at all, in very vague terms only. In *Romeo and Juliet*, III. 5. 42: ". . . one kiss, and I'll descend." In *Macbeth*, II. 2. 18: "As I descended." In *Antony and Cleopatra*, IV. 13. 13: "Help, friends below, let's draw him hither!" The reason for this vagueness is obvious: it would be awkward expressly to call the balcony on one occasion "a chamber" or "a promontory" when on another occasion shortly afterwards it has to serve as "a battlement" or "a ship at sea": the less clearly expressed, the better. This politic cautiousness of stage language has inevitably resulted in many doubts and queries.

Still, it should not be too difficult to find out what use Shakespeare made of the opportunity the double stage offered. In this inquiry we are helped (*a*) by the principle that "all pleasure consists in variety", as Dr. Johnson says. We may be sure that Shakespeare, being the dramatist he was, took the best possible advantage of the two-level stage. There is (*b*) the fact that Shakespeare the producer had to think of means how to mark the end of one scene and the beginning of another. He had no front-curtain; his chief method to indicate a break in the action was to use the two stages alternately. And there are (c) the texts of his scenes: they differ from one another, according to whether they are meant for the upper or lower stage.

*

I. I:

The soldiers and Horatio are on the lower stage. The Ghost makes his first appearance on the balcony. The second time he enters below, keeping to the background so that he can easily "vanish" behind the "arras", i.e., the curtain that separates the open stage from the "inner stage".

I. 2:

Lower stage. When King and Queen with their courtiers appear, there can be no doubt that the scene is no longer the "platform".

I. 3:

Laertes, Ophelia and later Polonius appear on the upper stage.

I. 4:

Lower stage. The Ghost emerges from behind the arras. Likewise, through the parting curtain, he disappears, followed by Hamlet.

I. 5:

First the Ghost and, shortly after him, Hamlet enter above. After the Ghost has gone, Horatio and Marcellus join Hamlet. The Ghost, speaking "under the stage", does so beneath the balcony, hidden from sight by the arras (see p. 45).

II. 1:

Lower stage.

II. 2:

Lower stage. Between the preceding and this scene no change of place is called for, nor is there any lapse of time.

III. 1:

Upper stage. At the beginning Polonius and Ophelia keep in the background. When Rosencrantz and Guildenstern have left and Claudius asks Gertrude to withdraw, ". . . for we have closely sent for Hamlet hither that he may here affront Ophelia," he points at the word "here" to the lower stage. Gertrude retires. Polonius hands Ophelia the prayer-book, and after: "We are oft to blame in this . . ." he dispatches his daughter; both disappear, she to go downstairs. Thus Claudius is alone for a while; which is necessary because of his short soliloquy: "O, 'tis too true! How smart a lash. . . ." After "O heavy burthen!" Polonius re-enters above, and with his line: "I hear him coming; let's withdraw, my lord!" they draw the halves of the curtain in front of the balcony, thus hiding themselves from sight. When Hamlet, on the lower stage, enters for his "To be or not to be . . .", he is to all appearance alone.

At the end of his soliloquy Ophelia enters, furnished

198

with the prayer-book and the "remembrances", which she has probably fetched in the meantime (or she would enter too early) and there is the "nunnery"-dialogue. At the end of this, Hamlet spies Polonius who in his super-curiosity peeps through the curtain, whereupon Hamlet, recognizing the situation, calls out: "Where's your father?"

Ophelia, left alone, has her soliloquy: "O, what a noble mind is here o'erthrown . . .", at the end of which she goes off to ascend the balcony. (Evidence for my conception seems to lie in the fact that Quarto 2 has actually after Ophelia's last words: ". . . see what I see" the stage-direction: "Exit".)

Meanwhile Polonius, having made sure that Hamlet has gone, draws the curtains aside. The King makes his speech: "Love? His affections . . .", to which Polonius replies. After his words: ". . . sprung from neglected love," Ophelia re-enters above in order to report, obedient daughter that she is, on her interview with Hamlet. Polonius says: "How now, Ophelia!"—the usual phrase to address a newcomer—and cuts her short: "You need not tell us . . . we heard it all."

III. 2:

Lower stage—with the exception of the Dumb-show, which is performed on the balcony (see pp. 42 ff).

III. 3:

Upper stage. When Rosencrantz and Guildenstern are dismissed and Polonius, too, has come and gone, Claudius has his soliloquy: "O, my offence is rank . . ."; after which he walks to one corner of the balcony, where he kneels in an attempt to pray. In the opposite corner Hamlet appears: "Now might I do it pat . . ." Having decided to spare his enemy for the time being, he goes off where he had come. Claudius rises and exit at the other side.

III. 4:

Lower stage. Polonius hides himself behind the arras. Gertrude and Hamlet have their altercation. He kills Polonius. The Ghost appears, and withdraws again. Hamlet exit, dragging Polonius behind the arras.

IV. 1:

This scene is a mere continuation of the preceding scene. Gertrude, left in tears, is joined by Claudius.

IV. 2:

Upper stage. Hamlet has "safely stowed" the body of Polonius, under "the stairs into the lobby". Rosencrantz and Guildenstern take the Prince as it were red-handed "in the lobby", and escort him downstairs.

IV. 3:

Lower stage.

IV. 4:

Lower stage. Fortinbras "with an Armie" marches towards Poland. (See Chapter X, p. 102.)

IV. 5:

Lower stage. When Gertrude with Horatio enters we are in no doubt as to where the scene takes place: in the palace again.

IV. 6:

Upper stage. In the preceding scene Horatio had been

sent off the stage; the King had told him to follow Ophelia.
Here now Horatio enters with a Servant; then the Sailors
bring him Hamlet's letters.

IV. 7:

Lower stage.

V. I:

Lower stage. The two Clowns enter. Their tools
(spades, ropes, etc.) and still more their discussion ("Is
she to be buried . . . make her grave straight . . .")
can leave no uncertainty about the locality of the scene.

v. 2, first part:

Upper stage. Hamlet and Horatio are joined by Osric.
When Hamlet accepts the invitation to the "fencing-match"
he does so with the words: "I will walk here in the hall. . .",
pointing to the lower stage. As to the Lord who (only in
Quarto 2) repeats the invitation, see p. 46.

v. 2, second part:

While downstairs the attendants bring in a table, the
rapiers, flagons of wine, chairs of state, etc., Hamlet and
Horatio descend from the balcony. At the same time the
royal couple with their followers enter below. The whole
of the remaining act takes place on the lower stage.

*

POSTSCRIPT

HAMLET never lived; nor did his father. Taking their stand on that undeniable fact, there are people, serious scholars among them, who find it ridiculous that they should inquire into the psychology of Shakespeare's characters. How ludicrous, they maintain, to bother about psychological background, motifs and motivations of beings who owe their whole existence—a paper existence —merely to a poet's imagination!

One could answer that Othello is more alive than any of us; that we know him better than any of our own brothers and friends; and that he will outlive any real person that really trod this earth.

"That may be so," my imaginary interlocutor might say: "but Othello's life is confined to that 'two hours' traffic', and at the end of the play he dies." Yes, he dies there, I should answer; but at the beginning of the play he is not a new-born babe. He enters it as a mature man, and in speaking, thinking and feeling he differs greatly from, say, Romeo or Hamlet. His past stretches into the present: he carries with him the full weight of his experience, and that weight makes him walk and behave with dignity and stateliness. Cleopatra, her supple limbs anointed with the oil of her amours, has emotions and emotional reactions which are different from those of Ophelia or Desdemona.

In fact, none of Shakespeare's characters can be cut off from his or her antecedents. The creatures of his imagination are not artificial flowers, made of velvet or leather and put in a glass bowl without water; they are flowers that have grown and developed, and continue to develop before our eyes. These flowers have stems and roots and

202

have sprung up from a soil that has been watered and manured, dug up and hoed as no other soil before. Manure cannot be sweet and clean; but the darker the ground, the whiter the lilies. It is true, though true only in the narrowest sense of the word, that Shakespeare's creations are not alive; but he who created them was; it is his blood and the irresistible throb of his great heart that makes them live.

All this is so self-evident that it needs no elaboration. Besides, a postscript should be brief. So I will take a short cut and bluntly put the question to which the foregoing paragraphs are meant to lead:

Can it be that in the Ghost's attitude towards Gertrude we are to recognize a trait of Shakespeare's own character? Is the Ghost's emotion an echo of his creator's emotion? Has Shakespeare clothed him with fabric taken from a page of his own psychological biography?

*

No author can convincingly depict emotions unless he has felt them himself, at least in a rudimentary measure. It is after all the profession of an actor to fill his own heart with the emotions he is to display. His texts show in every line that Shakespeare the *author* merely wrote what Shakespeare the *actor* had produced and approved, produced, i.e., during those silent first-nights on that invisible stage—"the stage behind his eyes," as I have called it elsewhere.* He himself had to feel Romeo's despair no less than Othello's blind wrath, Macbeth's gnawing ambition no less than Coriolanus's pride; and of each of those and so many more emotions there must have lain in the inmost recesses of his heart a tiny seed, or it could never have grown.

Grillparzer, the Austrian dramatist, maintained that

* *Shakespeare's Producing Hand*, Heinemann, 1948.

Shakespeare would have become a murderer himself had he not by creating those great criminals freed his own soul from that poisonous germ. Surely that is going too far? And yet, how could Shakespeare have visualized and called to life such characters as Shylock or Macbeth or Iago had he not, by some jinnee-like art, been able to creep as it were into their bodies, feel with their hearts and think with their brains?

Still——: love, hatred, vaulting ambition, contempt for the vulgar, vindictiveness, friendship, pity, pride, vanity, greed, envy, and innumerable other emotions can be produced and reproduced easily enough, especially by an actor, who is constantly training his soul as an acrobat trains his body. There is, moreover, the fact that for all those emotions and their various degrees, shades, and mixtures, there have always been patterns and types available to be studied and imitated, not only in life but in poetry also, from Homer to Æschylus, Plautus and Seneca. But if we are confronted with an emotion entirely of its own kind, completely new, with no parallel in previous literature, we are forced, I think, to look for its source in life. And in which life if not in that of the poet himself?

The Ghost's attitude towards Gertrude is truly unique. Never before has anything like it been described by any poet. The nearest approach I can think of is given in Richard Wagner's *Tristan und Isolde*; but King Mark, who endlessly repeats his disconsolate question: "Why? —why must this have happened to me?", what unmanly, tedious and larmoyant figure is he compared with Hamlet's father! King Hamlet had been betrayed by his wife; she was unfaithful to him with his own brother; he was murdered (to use a non-committal formula) in connection with that adultery; he had to leave this life "unaneled", with all his sins on his head; he is confined in purgatory, suffering tortures too dreadful to relate. And yet, when for one short hour he returns from his "prison-house", while doing everything to secure his revenge, he does everything to spare his wife any hurt, any grief, any humiliation. When his son is on the point of forcing her into admitting her own guilt, the Ghost intervenes in person, prevents her from humiliating herself and, with that "piteous action", not only forgives her on his own part but prevails on Hamlet to forgive her also. Surely to this attitude—of a cuckolded husband towards the adulteress—no parallel can be found in the literature of the world.

What is it that makes King Hamlet act as he does? Is it weakness? That cannot be, for as to the seducer he acts with the greatest severity. Is it Christian charity? an act of all-embracing forgiveness? Is it sexual thraldom, extending beyond temporal existence? Is it gratitude for a life of happiness? Is it all-enduring love in a "marriage of true minds" that refuses to alter "when it alteration finds?"

I am not bold enough to give an answer. I have, moreover, the feeling as if I were standing in front of a door which Shakespeare, were he alive, would not allow us to open—just as he forbade his bones to be moved:

GOOD FREND FOR IESUS SAKE FORBEARE,
TO DIGG THE DUST ENCLOASED HEARE:

Two things, however, I want to draw attention to. First, there is the fact that the Ghost's attitude towards Gertrude is not entirely isolated in Shakespeare's work. Othello, too, is—in his imagination—a betrayed husband. He is about to kill his wife for her unfaithfulness. And yet, on the very bed on which he smothers her a few minutes later he kisses her—because even now, bent on murder, he cannot but love her.

The second point is the existence of a series of Sonnets

in which similar sentiments are expressed. In the Sonnets 58, 120, in 133 and 134 footprints can be discovered that seem to fit the Ghost's feet. In 135 the poet tries to poke fun, grimly bitter fun, at an "eternal-triangle" situation. And in the 150th Sonnet we find that outcry—truly the outcry of a tortured soul—that might have been uttered by King Hamlet and Othello alike:

Who taught thee how to make me love thee more,
The more I hear and see just cause of hate?

What had Shakespeare gone through, through what agonies of desecrated love? By what passion was he possessed which he had not the strength to cut out of his heart? What humiliations had he endured unable to set himself free? In what "prison-house", in what purgatory had he been confined?

We do not know. Whatever it was, it was a tragedy. We should not try to lift the curtain of oblivion that has dropped on it.

INDEX